Tired of Crying

From the Stripper House to the Church House

By
Kessan Mandolph

iUniverse LLC
Bloomington

Tired of Crying
From the Stripper House to the Church House

iUniverse books may be ordered through booksellers or by contacting:

iUniverse LLC
1663 Liberty Drive
Bloomington, IN 47403
www.iuniverse.com
1-800-Authors (1-800-288-4677)

Because of the dynamic nature of the Internet, any web addresses or links contained in this book may have changed since publication and may no longer be valid. The views expressed in this work are solely those of the author and do not necessarily reflect the views of the publisher, and the publisher hereby disclaims any responsibility for them.

Any people depicted in stock imagery provided by Thinkstock are models, and such images are being used for illustrative purposes only.
Certain stock imagery © Thinkstock.

ISBN: 978-1-4759-6607-7 (sc)
ISBN: 978-1-4759-6608-4 (ebk)

Printed in the United States of America

iUniverse rev. date: 08/06/2013

CONTENTS

In Loving Memory iv

Dedication v

Acknowledgments vi

Introduction... vii

Chapter One: My Journey in Life 1

Chapter Two: How Could This Happen? 30

Chapter Three: Who's that Girl?..49

Chapter Four: A Different Me! 59

Chapter Five: The Transition 71

Chapter Six: Why Him? 90

Chapter Seven: The Completion 118

Chapter Eight: The Battle Is Not Yours; It's the Lord's......... 148

In Loving Memory
of
James Ray Sconiers, III
"Indy"

October 11, 1992-January 14, 1996

"Hakuna Matata"

Celebrating the Homegoing of
James Ray Sconiers, III ("Indy")
Sunrise—October 11, 1992
Sunset—January 14, 1996

Monday, January 22, 1996—1:30 p.m.
Corner-Johnson Mortuary
4700 South Avalon Blvd
Los Angeles, CA

DEDICATION

I dedicate this book to my spiritual parents, Pastor Sanders White, Sr., and Sister Annie White. Giving all glory and honor to the Most High God for determining even before I was gifted to my natural mother that these two amazing people would stand in the gap on my behalf, take me under their wings, love, teach, and even sometimes correct me as if I was their natural-born daughter. I often find it hard to put into words all that I feel for them in my heart.

Pastor and Sister White: I thank you for all you have done for me, for being here for me, for loving me, and accepting me for me. Thank you for all the wisdom, prayers, and life lessons you have so willingly poured out and taught. Truly, I know without a shadow of a doubt that I would not be where I am today, nor would this book have been possible, had I not been obedient to the call of God where you two are concerned. I love you and thank God for you!

ACKNOWLEDGMENTS

To my loving and supportive sisters,
I love and thank you all for being here for me.

To my wonderful children,
Keithshon and Jamie,
I love you more than words can say.

INTRODUCTION

I am writing this book for anyone who is currently struggling with personal obstacles in life. My purpose for sharing with you my story of pain, grief, abuse, and loss is to encourage you so you will know that it can and will get better in time.

The first time I entered El Shaddai Christian church, Pastor Sanders White, Sr., and his family embraced me. They took me under their wings. Throughout my own personal transition, they remained with me, although there were things about me and my life which they certainly did not agree with. Instead of judging me, they continued to show the unconditional love parents would show their own daughter. I was never made to feel bad about my past or the decisions I had made because of my life experiences. Instead, they continued to remind me just how much God loves me, assuring me that everything would be okay if I put all of my trust in Him.

Writing this story was not an easy thing to do. What I will share is a series of events I experienced, beginning in childhood. I would like to help others who will read this book, especially those who may be in the same position that I was. Some people may not be able to accept what I have written, but I must write the truth in order to be free to move on to my next assignment in my life. I know that God has great things in store for me and my children. I gave up my life for my children—Lady Bug and Keithshon. I would certainly do it all over again. I have changed some of the names of individuals and places because I don't want to give glory to negativity. I also must state that God's grace is eternal, and I pray that He will change the hearts of those who may have done wrong in the past. I'd like to avoid eternally "villainizing" these individuals and will continue to pray for them.

I know that God is taking my son down his own path right now, and I want him to know that Mommy loves him. One day my son will stand up, take his rightful place in God's Kingdom, and become the man that God is calling him to be. I will never give up on my son or my daughter. I know without a doubt that God saved both of you in that fire for a reason. You will see and understand more as you grow older.

I cannot guarantee that this book I've written about my life's journey thus far will attain worldly success. I do know that God has already granted me a huge spiritual reward for my obedience in placing paper to pen. I hope that everyone who reads this book will continue to stand and trust in God for the right path to take. I pray that my story helps to encourage.

Tired of Crying

Chapter One:
My Journey in Life

ALL I EVER WANTED WAS TO BE LOVED.

Whether it was from my mother, my father, or the man who would beat me until the blood flowed from my nose and dried up like a forgotten plum that fell too soon from its tree, I was always seeking love. I could never figure out what was wrong with me. Why every person I tried to love never loved me back. I cooked, cleaned, and loved them in every way that was asked of me. I even did more than what was expected. Each and every time, I did so much more than what was expected, but none of them was ever faithful to me. Eventually, they all left me . . . alone! Initially, they would make me believe that it was my fault that they were leaving me, which made me feel like curling up into a ball and dying.

Erma Mandolph is my mother's name. Many of the memories of her that I still carry with me are based upon what I have been told. I was told that my mother abused drugs almost her entire short life, even when she was pregnant with me. Her choice of poison was heroin.

My name is Kessan Mandolph and this is my story. I was born on August 16, 1975, the day my crazy journey in life began. I'm told that my mother left me in a hotel room with a stranger for three days. Thankfully, Beverly, my godmother, rescued me from that situation and took me to live with my Aunt Bert. Aunt Bert was my mother's youngest sister, who eventually raised me and my siblings. When I was picked up from that hotel room, I was clothed in nothing except a towel that covered my bottom. I was told that my mother had been so high on drugs that she had forgotten all about me—and I was only a week old at the time.

I remember having a pretty good childhood. Aunt Bert was already raising my other siblings: Yolanda, the eldest, Angie and Andrea, the twins, my sister Christina, who is just a little older than me, and my brother Jermaine, the only boy in the bunch. We were all together. We lived in a good neighborhood, attended the best schools, and had the nicest clothes. I never really paid much attention to the fact that my mother wasn't around. My mother never really had to take care of her children. She would have my brother and sisters for a while, but would eventually leave them in the house alone, and Aunt Bert would come to the rescue. It was for this reason that Aunt Bert took all of us and raised us herself.

I do remember living with my mother for approximately two years when I was about four. During that time, we stayed on Hillcrest in "The Jungle," in South Los Angeles. Although I was very young, I can still remember lying in the bed with my sisters and brother listening to the loud music while mom was drinking and partying. Like any other child, I was always curious about what was going on around me. When no one was looking, I would peek around the corner to see people sitting on the couch. I could see them drinking, smoking, kissing, talking, laughing, and gambling. It didn't take Aunt Bert long to figure out that this was not the best life for me.

I went to live with mom again when I was about six years old; once again, this had to come to an end. When Aunt Bert came to get me, I was so ready to leave my mother's house. I knew that I would be back where life was peaceful again. I recall the things that made my childhood great, from the water balloon fights I would have with my sister Marchelle (who is really my cousin, Aunt Bert's only child) to the stories she would read faithfully to me whenever I couldn't fall asleep.

My favorite memories of my childhood are listening to music and waking up to the smell of bacon, eggs, and pancakes that filled my room. My aunt would wake up at the crack of dawn to make all of us breakfast on Sunday mornings. I remember being in a deep sleep in my bed which was a pullout bunk that was at the bottom of Eva's daybed. I would open my eyes and sit up to see if she was still asleep on top but, as always, she would already be up in the living room, sitting on the couch watching television, waiting to eat. I would roll out of my bed, grab my robe, and wander into the kitchen. I would sit at the table and watch my aunt sing her Pattie LaBelle songs and cook for us. I loved listening to our favorite songs, singing and dancing around the house until we passed out from laughing. Don't get me wrong, Aunt Bert was also very strict, especially when it came to me.

Although Aunt Bert raised me, I had my mom's fighting spirit. Looking back, I can still remember the many times she would come home huffing and puffing, hands bloody from her fighting. She raised her children to fight, too. Mom had one son, and I'm sure she loved him just as much as her girls, but she took pride in passing on the talent for fighting to her daughters.

One time, during one of my visits to her house, she got into scuffle with another woman. Shurlie was my mother's best friend, and they liked to get high together. On this particular day, my mom came into the house late in the evening—she was high and tired. Shurlie wanted to come inside to use the bathroom, so she banged on the door screaming for my mom to open the door. For some reason, my mom wouldn't let her in. Suddenly, Shurlie stood in front of the big picture window, right in the front yard, and pulled her panties down and urinated right there! Shurlie, angry and out of control, threw a brick hard and busted the window.

Groggy and upset by the loud noise, my mom stormed out of the room to investigate. As the twins and I followed her, she saw the broken window. She immediately knew who was responsible. My mother jumped right through the window and chased her down. When my mother caught up to her, she beat Shurlie up badly. But that wasn't a rare thing. We were accustomed to our mom doing crazy stuff like that, so it didn't seem unusual for this to happen. This story is just one of many.

From the ages of eight to twelve, I was a great kid. My grades were good, and I often stayed in the house watching old movies with my sisters. But as time went on and puberty started, my hormones started racing. I discovered boys and how they noticed me. Since I wasn't allowed to hang out with them, I started sneaking out. It was all very innocent at first. I would go inside when the lights came on, like I was supposed to, then later, I would sneak out to meet boys. We would meet at the movies or the park with some of my other friends. It was all just teenage fun, or so I thought. As time went on, however, I started to change for the worse.

Being responsible and excelling in school no longer appealed to me. I started hanging around the wrong crowd just to fit in. I had also become pretty popular, largely due to my bad attitude and lack of respect for my elders. Early on, I realized that I got more attention for behaving badly than for doing the right things. Looking back, I now realize I was just expressing the issues resulting from my childhood. My habit of fighting, seemingly passed down from my mother, led to frequent trips to the principal's office. Eventually, my aunt grew tired of coming to the school for conferences or to pick me up after I had been suspended for bad behavior. "I'm never coming back up to this school again," she finally said. "If they want to kick you out, they should just go ahead and do it!"

My behavior had really gotten out of hand. I didn't listen to my aunt at home, either. Back then, I was also known for being as rude as I was uncooperative. Since I was not allowed to have boyfriends, I hid from my family the fact that I had begun dating this guy I had known for a month. He name was Brad and I was so smitten by his walk and his talk. At the beginning, we were only able to spend time together before and after school. One day we were walking to the bus stop with some of our friends, joking and clowning around, when suddenly a group of about fifteen other teenagers came around the corner in our direction. None of us paid much attention to them until they stopped right in front us.

A girl in the crowd asked my boyfriend why he was hanging out with me. There was something about the look on his face that led me to believe that I was in grave danger. He was upset, and told her that it was none of her business who he talked to or hung out with since they weren't together anymore. The girl got angry and decided that she was not going to let some other girl come between the two of them. It turned out that she was a big-time gangbanger who was determined to teach me a lesson. After their exchange, everything started to happen very quickly. Two of her friends pushed him away from me, and the girl along with five of her friends jumped me, leaving me banged up pretty bad. Eventually, I was able to fight my way out of the crowd, and I ran away, hopping on the first bus that arrived.

Because I came from a family of fighters, I knew that what happened to me was not over, at least not until my sisters proved that no one messed with me. And because my mother was also a former gang member and my twin sisters were still affiliated with one, this was just another day in the hood to them. The big confrontation and subsequent fight happened on that Friday. On Monday, right after school, I came outside and found three cars full of my family members sitting out in front. They called me over and made me get into one of the cars.

We were ready for action, driving around for about an hour to find the place where the girl and her friends were known to hang out. Right before we were going to give up the search, we spotted them in a parking lot. My anger began to increase at the sight of them. I got out of the car and approached the main girl who had jumped me. As I walked through the crowd, she started to back up, but I knew I wasn't going to let her leave. As she tried to run through the crowd, to my surprise her own friends closed her in so that she couldn't run. I took a swing at her and we started to fight, but this time it was one on one, and I was so happy to have this moment. I beat her until I could see the blood running from her face. My family grabbed me and pulled me off her. Apparently, someone had called the police because the sirens were getting closer and closer. I had to make it clear to her that I was not the one to be challenged again, and I was finally satisfied that we had come to an understanding. At least I had, and I thought the entire ordeal was over, but that wasn't the case.

A few days later, I found myself backed into a corner by some of her friends on the schoolyard during recess. I was running out of options quickly, and from experience, I knew the only way to come out of this situation was swinging, which is exactly what I did! In the process, one of the girls was stabbed with the pencil I was clutching in my left hand. I ended up in the principal's office once again, ultimately expelled for my involvement in an incident that caused bodily injury to another person. Audubon was the first school I was kicked out of for fighting, but it wouldn't be the last. My poor Aunt Bert was trying to deal with me and was quickly getting weary of me being hardheaded, back talking, and my lack of interest in school. Along with that, my grades had started to drop significantly and I didn't even care.

To make matters worse, a young man named Kevin Meade, a handsome, high-yellow, curly-haired guy, invited himself into my world. He was twenty-two and I was fifteen—a recipe for disaster! Although I didn't get to see him that often, I made every minute count when I did. When it would start to get late and I knew I had to get home, he would hold and kiss me in a way that made my body speak a language that I couldn't even begin to understand. All I could hear in those stolen moments was him pleading for me to stay a little while longer. "If you love me, you won't leave." I stayed, allowing myself to leave the world I had known and journey into his, thinking that I was now safe and secure. Two months later, I had fallen into a steady routine, which included spending as much time with Kevin as I possibly could, getting accustomed to a new school, and making new friends.

One Thursday afternoon, my best friend Maggie and I were in my room listening to our favorite CD. Suddenly I had to run to the bathroom and made it just in time to start puking my brains out into the toilet. At first, I thought I was catching a virus, but I had also missed my period for the second time, and realized that the worst thing in the world had just happened to me. I was fifteen and pregnant.

For the first few months, I tried to hide it. Trying hard not to think past each day, I wore big clothes, kept to myself, and went straight to my room when I got home. On the weekends, I would stay at Maggie's house since she was also secretly expecting her first child. This arrangement made it a lot easier for us to comfort each other. Her parents didn't have a clue about her situation either.

As my pregnancy advanced, I started to ditch school to hang out with my child's father. He was always doing something illegal, which made it difficult for me as a fifteen-year-old child, who was supposed to be at school during school hours, to be discreet and unnoticed. When I was with him, it drew a great deal of attention, so I decided to go back to school.

I was still keeping the big secret. Every waking moment all I could think about was, *How in the world am I going to tell my family?* When I couldn't hide it any longer, I revealed my secret to my sister, Eva. I gathered the nerve to tell her and I sat on the couch in the living room, holding my head down, struggling to find the right words to say. Unable to watch me much longer, she blurted out, "I already know; I was just waiting for you to tell me." As we looked into each other's eyes, silent tears streamed down my face. I knew she was very disappointed in me. She told me that I was much too young to have a child, and that she would call and make me an appointment to "take care of it."

I can remember standing in front of the clinic with my sisters, Eva, Andrea, Christina, and my boyfriend Kevin. Andrea kept talking to me about what I should say and do, but I wasn't listening. I was too confused to hear anything she was saying, except that she repeated over and over, "If they ask you if you are being forced to do this, you have to say, 'No!'" As soon as I was behind the closed door of the examining room, I broke down crying telling the doctor that I really didn't want to go through with the abortion. With no other choice, they released me and told my family that they were unable to perform the procedure.

When we arrived home, we went straight into the living room where my aunt was sitting on the couch waiting. Wasting no time, she asked Eva what happened at the clinic. Reluctantly, she informed Aunt Bert that I had refused to terminate my pregnancy and nothing else could be done. Soon afterwards, everyone left except for Kevin. We just sat in the living room discussing the matter with Eva and my aunt. We wanted to decide realistically how to proceed. Aunt Bert believed in tough love. She knew from experience that the only way we would ever learn some of life's hardest lessons was for us to walk our own path, so she told me to leave. Since I wanted to act grown up, I most certainly couldn't play house living under her roof. I should, "Let that grown man who knocked you up take care of you guys." In my fifteen-year-old wisdom, I thought this was great! I would live with the man who I thought I was in love with, raise our baby together, and live this wonderful life.

As I walked away with my bags, I felt this sharp, aching pain in my chest. Sad and teary-eyed, the thought of leaving my aunt hit me like a ton of bricks. I was leaving my family, all that I had known. Momentarily petrified with fear, I knew that I wasn't ready to grow up and be on my own. I also knew that it was too late. The decision had been made and I couldn't turn back. So I just sucked it up and thought, *Hey, he got me pregnant; he wants to have the baby! At least, that's what he told me.* I convinced myself that he was going to take care of me. I thought he would keep me safe. Boy was I wrong.

Even after I left my aunt's house, I kept going to school for a while. I really didn't have a place to stay because consistent housing was our biggest challenge. School became nearly impossible. Kevin would go to his favorite hangouts and hustle up money for us to get a hotel room, but it wasn't a consistent source of income. On nights that he couldn't get enough money to rent a room, we would sleep in a friend's car. In the mornings, we would wait for her mom to leave for work. I would go into the house, take a shower, and head off to school. Kevin would hit the streets to get his hustle on. This routine only lasted a few months. Eventually I gave up going to school all together, finding other ways to keep busy until we met up each evening.

One day, Kevin came up with a lot of money. I never knew how much or where he got it from. Nevertheless, we were able to rent a hotel room for weeks at a time. Every night, after a long day of activity, he would bring back food for dinner. One time, I woke up alone and looked around for him, but he had apparently left earlier. I got up and made the bed while trying to figure out my next move. To my surprise, I found two thousand dollars under his pillow. For the next two days, all I did was watch TV, eat, and wait for a little bit of darkness so I would have a reason to fall asleep. By the time he made it back to the hotel, I was so wrung-out and exhausted from crying and pacing the floor all night that I forgot all about the money as soon as he came walking through the door. Looking back, I have to admit that I was just happy he had come back to get me at all. This was the first of many times that I'd be left alone.

As time went on, things between us started to get really bad. Kevin stayed away for longer periods and gave no explanations when he did come back. Our motel stay ended abruptly when he came in after being away for three days and told me to pack up all our stuff in a hurry. We had to leave right then and we weren't coming back. I had no clue why we had to leave in such a hurry, but I did as I was told and didn't ask the nagging questions forming at the back of my mind. We had run out of money and could no longer afford to pay for the hotel room, so we took the bus headed to Hollywood. That was the place he went to meet his friends and make his money. Later, I discovered that he actually made his money by prostituting women.

When we arrived in Hollywood, we went to a fast-food restaurant where Kevin told me to stay inside, saying he would be back shortly after making a phone call. I sat at the third table, close to the door so I would be able to see him when he came back to get me. I really didn't want people to see me waiting there because I was so hungry. Watching people buy food only made my hunger that much more intense and hard to ignore. I secretly hoped that someone would see the hungry look in my eyes and offer me something to eat. I was too embarrassed for them to know that I was hungry and hurting at the same time.

When people did make eye contact with me, I would look away quickly. They were probably wondering why a teenage girl was sitting in this place wearing big pants and an oversized T-shirt. My hair wasn't combed and I knew I looked a mess. Maybe they thought that I was homeless in Hollywood. As I sat there feeling lonely, lost, and scared, I just couldn't figure out how I had gotten in this situation. How did my life turn out like this? It suddenly hit me that I had been sitting there a very long time and Kevin had yet to return for me.

Beginning to panic, I went outside and looked around. I went to the corner and walked back and forth, searching for any sign of him. It felt like I was standing still in a movie. People were moving all around me and staring right through me. I wanted to run and hide but I had nowhere to go. Unsure of what to do, I went back to the restaurant and sat down for a few minutes. I was torn between fear, a resolve to wait for Kevin, and being ready to flee, but I didn't dare leave just in case he came back and couldn't find me. Sick with anxiety, I finally figured out he wasn't coming back for me after all. I felt my world crashing down around me and began to cry. I really didn't want anyone to see me like that, so I tried to remain calm.

I went outside and cried. I didn't know what to do, but I knew I certainly couldn't go home to my Aunt Bert. I was desperate, so I called my friend, Tejuana, who picked me up. As we drove away in her car, I remember staring out the window thinking, *Wow! I'm pregnant, I'm homeless, and I'm scared and hungry. What am I going to do?* Because I had no place to sleep, she let me sleep in her car. A guy she was dating allowed her to park the car in front of his house. Truthfully, I felt more at peace sleeping in that car than I had staying in a hotel room with Kevin for the past few months. When we arrived at her boyfriend's house, I sat up thinking, trying to figure out what I was going to do about my situation. What I knew was that I wouldn't be able to stay there long, especially since she wasn't even supposed to be there in the first place.

The next morning, she gave me some food and we discussed my options. It was a long conversation and I decided it would be best for me to go to a maternity home. She suggested that I put myself in the system under the court's authority. Later that evening, my friend told me about Saint Ann's Maternity Home, a girls' home managed by nuns who provided boarding services to unwed teenage mothers-to-be. Tejuana thought that I should check it out, and since I had no other options, I did. When I called the office, I was told that they were closed. I could either call back or just come in the next morning.

The process wasn't as hard as I thought. I told them that I was homeless and needed a place to stay. They gave me some paperwork that I completed, and the next thing I knew I was being led to a room that I shared with another girl. There was a large shower room for everyone, except for the girls whose parents paid for them to stay there. Those were the girls who had their own room with a private bathroom and shower. There were approximately fifty girls living at Saint Ann's Maternity Home. All of us were required to attend school, do our own laundry once a week, and on Fridays, if all of our chores were done, each of us would receive twenty-five dollars. We were allowed to leave for the weekend, as long as we were back at the home on Sundays by six p.m. I soon settled into my new room, and things were going well. Somehow, Kevin found out where I was and began visiting every weekend. We started talking on the phone every night. It seemed like he wanted to be part of our lives and I was happy to be with him again. But things aren't always what they seem.

One Sunday, when I returned home from a weekend away, I was stopped before I could go into my room by Sara, a girl I had become friends with. She told me that Kevin was there on Saturday, but not to visit me. He had actually come to visit another girl, and had been doing so for a couple of weeks. She also told me that they talked on the phone right after he and I usually hung up from speaking with each other. At that moment, I remembered that a few days prior, two of the girls who stayed down the hall were standing at the door whispering and rolling their eyes at me. I didn't pay it much attention because I knew if I put too much energy into it, I would have laid both of them out on the floor right where they stood.

I immediately tried to call Kevin and didn't get an answer, so I just went downstairs for dinner and decided to try again later. After dinner, I took a shower and remembered that I still needed to contact Kevin. While using the phone booth located next to the recreation room, the same girls who were standing at the end of the hall rolling their eyes came over to me and started yelling and cussing at me, telling me to get off the phone with her man, and trying to yank open the phone booth door. I was on the phone with Kevin by this time, trying to get answers about what I'd just discovered. I put the phone down, stepped outside of the phone booth, and walked up on her. We started arguing back and forth. The argument escalated, then I grabbed one of the girls by the hair and slammed her on the floor. After the nuns came to investigate, they took me into the office and said it would be better for everyone if I called somebody to come to pick me up. They wanted me to go somewhere else, just until some of the tension in the house eased up. I called my sisters to pick me up. Of course they were upset by the call, but after speaking to the nuns, my sisters calmed down and we left together.

When I came back to Saint Ann's, I had a meeting with the nuns and we agreed that I should leave permanently since this was not the first time I had been singled out for harassment by this group of girls. When I'd first arrived at the home, these same girls wanted the room I was assigned because it was the only one with a view of the rose garden. Ever since that incident there was a problem with this group, not to mention one of the girls was involved with Kevin. After talking it over with my family, we decided the best course of action was for me to go live with my sister Christina.

The decision to go live with Christina definitely wasn't my first choice, but it was the only viable option at the time. I made up my mind to swallow my pride and make the best of it. Things were going well at first, even though I hadn't heard from Kevin since I'd left Saint Ann's. I decided to get myself together for my child, so I enrolled myself back into Dorsey High School since I had stopped going soon after my pregnancy, and I also began looking for a job. I was about six months pregnant and it wasn't as easy as I thought it would be. No one wanted to hire an underage pregnant teenager who would be a liability to the company, so I just gave up.

When I was bored, I would go for walks just to get out of the house. One day I was walking to the store and just enjoying the sunshine. Out of the blue, this guy pulled up behind me trying to get my attention, but I just kept walking. I began to see him every day, the same guy, in this old truck which reminded me of the show *Sanford and Son,* and he would follow right behind me.

A week after this began, I was walking to the laundry mat to wash my clothes and I saw him sitting on his porch talking with his friend. Avoiding eye contact, I kept walking until he ran after me and told me his name was Jesse. He asked if he could take me wherever I was going because I shouldn't be carrying all these bags of clothes by myself. I was hesitant at first, but I really didn't want to walk five blocks to do my laundry so I told him it was okay to take me to the laundry mat.

From that day on, Jesse and I hung out almost every day. I couldn't understand why this guy was so nice to me. I mean, I was carrying another man's child, but that didn't seem to bother him at all. He would make sure I ate every day, took me to every doctor's appointment, and even dropped me off at school. My sister Christina got along well with Jesse because whenever he would do something for me, he made sure that she had whatever she needed as well.

He never let anyone disrespect me. I remember one time when his daughter's mom was sitting in front of my house in her car. She was sitting there because she wanted to know who was the new girl in his life. Before I could come outside, Jesse pulled her out of her car and threw her on the hood of it. He told her she was never to come to my house again or he wouldn't be so nice the next time. There was another time when he went off on some girls on his mother's block (where he lived as well) because they were talking to me crazy. They were sisters and one of the older girls liked him so, of course, they weren't too fond of me.

While sitting in the car in front of his house one day, the eldest sister, who lived five houses down from him on the same side of the street, was walking by making smart remarks to me. Although I just ignored her, for some reason Jesse wouldn't let it go. He looked over at me while we were sitting in the car, told me that I needed to handle her, and to get out the car and whip her a**. I was seven-and-a-half-months pregnant, but for some reason this didn't matter to him or me either. The only reason the fight was broken up was his older sister came out of the house and stopped it. After that, everyone knew I was his girl and never messed with me again. I thought I was so safe with him. Once again, I would soon discover I was wrong.

Living with Christina was not always easy. At one point, she put me out of the house at two in the morning. I was lying on the couch in the small living room in the house we lived in. It was behind our grandmother's house. It was a one-bedroom, back house, and I slept on the couch located closest to the front door. Christina came in, slammed the door, went straight to her room, and started fussing. She was frustrated over a disagreement she'd had with her boyfriend earlier that day; I knew that it wasn't going to be a good night. Still angry, she came into the living room and inquired if I had been on her house phone. Apparently, she was trying to call but the phone had been busy for at least an hour. I said, "No," rolled over, and went back to sleep. Still mad, she told me I was being disrespectful by turning my back to her. Not satisfied, she snatched the covers off me.

I sat up and said to her, "Please don't start!"

"I can do whatever I like," she told me. 'This is my house and if you don't like it you can get out!"

My mom was there, and came inside the living room saying, "Chill, you guys!"

Pissed off at the interruption, Christina started fussing and cussing at our mother. Our mom told her that she was tripping and went back to her room, which was a storage space in the back of the house. She closed the door and left me alone with my sister. Christina started venting again and said that she was tired of coming into the house and dealing with my stuff. I don't even remember the whole story because it was two o'clock in the morning and I was tired.

I told her, "I don't want to hear this. Can I please go back to sleep?"

Enraged by my lack of concern, she kept fussing until I finally got up, and we started arguing back and forth. Fed up with me, Christina told me to get out of her house if I was going to be disrespectful. I was tired and angry, so I gave up fighting with her and walked out. At that moment, I didn't really care. I left her house, walked to the end of the corner, and saw Jesse's truck. He wasn't sitting inside it so I knew that he was in the house asleep. Because I didn't have a cell phone, I sat down on the sidewalk at the corner and tried to calm down.

Shortly after the argument, Christina's boyfriend Moe came over and talked to her, and told her she was wrong. She was still too angry to give in, so my mom walked down the street and knocked on the back bedroom window where Jesse slept. She told him what had happened so he let me sleep in his truck because sleeping in his mother's house was not an option. The next morning, I snuck into my sister's house when she left for work. When she came home that evening, she did not acknowledge my presence or the fact that she had been fussing at me just hours before, and that was okay. I knew that it was Christina's way of showing me that she felt bad about what she had done to me the night before.

It was a Wednesday morning. I was lying on the couch and Jesse was lying next to me because he had spent the night. Awakened by a persistent pressure in my stomach, I sat up and told him I needed to go to the bathroom. When I returned, I told Jesse that I was still feeling the pressure. He called for my mom who was sleeping in the next room. She had been out all night, doing what she had always done—abusing drugs and hanging out. Responding to the urgency in Jesse's voice, my mom came into the living room and quickly determined that I was, in fact, in labor. Her high did not override her motherly instincts; she told me to get up and get dressed. From that point on, taking charge, she called Christina, who was at her boyfriend's house, informing her that it was time for me to go to the hospital.

Anxious and excited, I took a shower, got dressed, and threw on a t-shirt, sweats, and tennis shoes. In the meantime, Jesse went home to shower and change his clothes. When we arrived at the hospital, I was checked in, given a wristband, and escorted to my delivery room. Once there, I changed into a hospital gown and got into my hospital bed. The nurse came in to take my blood pressure and hooked me up to a machine that monitored the baby's heart rate. At first, I thought having a baby would be a breeze—until the contractions began and I lost my mind!

My mom was right there with me the whole time. Later on, my sisters arrived and kept me company while my mother went downstairs to get something to eat. She was only gone for twenty minutes but soon returned to the room to tell jokes as if she had never left. She was always a jokester, so when she said to me, "I bet your a** you wish you would have waited now," it was also her way of showing me comfort. I tried to laugh and play it off, but I just couldn't do it. I was in a lot of pain and I was crying.

I asked my mom to find a truck to run me over with because the pain was so unbearable. My mom told me, "You'll be alright! You'll get through it. You can't turn back now." I couldn't lie down, sit up, eat, or drink anything, and to top it all off, some nurse came in telling me that she needed to give me an enema to clean me out. At this point, I was climbing out the bed, trying to leave.

Jesse finally got there just as I was about to go into the delivery room. The labor itself was much harder than I could have ever imagined. I pushed and pushed for about thirty minutes, finally feeling a pop, which quickly released the pressure I was feeling. Then I heard him crying. I was so excited when they said, "It's a boy!" Keithshon was six pounds, eight ounces, and totally adorable. I had never felt such an all-consuming love like this before. The best part was my mom stayed with me and talked me through all of my contractions until it was time for me to deliver. It was a rare occasion. She was there for me as a mother and I savored every moment of it.

His birth was a special time for me. I was in my room resting when my family came to visit me. I was really surprised to see my sister Eva. We were very close when I lived with my aunt, but she was so disappointed when I got pregnant that she didn't really speak to me the whole time. Despite that, she came to the hospital and brought clothes; she even bought her new nephew a car seat. When she came into the room, she just looked at me like, "No matter what you do, you can never disappoint me so much that I won't be there to support you." I was so elated when I saw her come through the door. I decided to name Keithshon after her, and my older sister, Yolanda. Keithshon Marcell Dewan Meade. When we received the paperwork for the birth certificate, she was standing right there. I asked her if she would do me the honor of being his godmother. She was so happy! That was the best decision I've ever made.

Kevin came to see our baby once, when he was two weeks old, bringing his father along just to see if our son was really his. After that day, I didn't think about Kevin that much. I was living a good life. I had given birth to a gorgeous, healthy baby boy. My relationship with my sister Christina was even getting better. I told her that I would try to find my own place when Keithshon was older. Although she and I were getting along, Christina and Jesse didn't seem to get along anymore for some strange reason. She would start a fight with me every time he came over to visit and, of course, this started the tension between her and me once again. I had been living with Christina for seven months.

After giving birth to Keithshon, I was supposed to go back to school; I did home study instead. I remained focused on my studies despite everything that was going on around me. My mom continued getting high, and Christina was always coming in the house fussing and cussing about anything she could find to fuss and cuss about. Every day things got worse. My sister would call me a bad mom for taking Keithshon with me down the street to visit Jesse. She even called the caseworker assigned to me when I left the maternity home and told her that I had left Keithshon in the house alone! The truth was she'd put me out of her house, refusing to let me back in until two days later. Christina also argued a lot with Jesse, which led to her decision that he was never allowed back in her house again.

After that, my life really started to get crazy. My sister and I fought with each other almost every day. I was frustrated and I knew I couldn't stay there much longer. The only thing on my mind was where was I going to live. I tried to stay away from her house as much as I could. My sister put a stop to that when she called my caseworker again, this time announcing that I couldn't stay there anymore because I was causing too much trouble.

That same day my social worker called to inform me that she had found a foster home for me and would pick me up at four p.m. My mom came down to Jesse's house and gave me the message. She said that I should go home to start getting my things together. At first, I was going to wait for my caseworker. I knew that if I went down to Christina's house things wouldn't turn out well. I decided to go to the house anyway and pack up all of my belongings. To my surprise, and embarrassment, my sister had put all my stuff outside on the porch. The baby's crib was broken into pieces and our clothing thrown all over the yard. When I saw this, my blood rushed to the front of my brain. The next thing I knew, I was charging at her like a bull. I grabbed her by the hair and we started to fight. Jesse was sitting in front of the house and heard all the commotion. He came running to break up the fight.

By that time, Christina had broken away and locked herself in the house. I was so upset at what she had done that I was completely out of control. I saw her standing in front of the window, still talking crazy to me from inside, so I picked up a big can of baby formula that she had thrown in the yard and hurled it at the window with all of my strength. The can merely bounced off the window. Frankly, I threw it so hard, it should have shattered that entire window. As Jesse dragged all of my things to the front of the yard, I sat on the curb and waited for the next two hours until my social worker pulled up to take me to my new home.

My new home wasn't far from where Jesse lived, which made it easy for him to visit me daily to make sure I was doing okay. My foster family consisted of an older couple, Mr. and Mrs. Henderson, who owned and managed the building in which they lived. The Hendersons were also raising their granddaughter, Nikki, who was also in the system.

I had my own bedroom, which made me really happy, especially because I had been through so much in the past year. All I wanted was a room of my own where I could go and hide from the rest of the world. This place was perfect because whenever I was in my room, my foster parents never bothered me. My room was located at the end of the hallway and Nikki's room was in the middle. In my room, there was a bed, a television and the baby's crib. The only thing I hated was going into the kitchen where Mr. Henderson, a heavy-set man who liked sitting at the counter and reading the paper with his shirt off, spent a lot of his time. I never really liked how he looked at me whenever I entered the kitchen.

We were required to buy our own food with the government assistance I was receiving, which was fine. The money allowed me to purchase groceries. Normally, I would keep the dry food in my room and put the cold food in the family refrigerator. I hated to go into that kitchen because Mr. Henderson would be sitting there watching me. I would always catch him staring at my body in such a disgusting manner, which always sent chills up and down my spine. I dreaded the thought of being alone with him. I made sure that I was fully dressed whenever he was around so he wouldn't give me those nasty looks that I hated.

The arrangement was better than being at Christina's, but I was never quite comfortable there anyway. Besides, I already knew I wasn't staying for long because Jesse was out looking for a place for us to live. The plan was for me to run away from the foster home when Jesse found a place. He continued to visit every day and we were doing really well; but it didn't last long. It never did.

Early one evening I was sitting outside with Keithshon talking to my friend Annie who stayed in one of the apartments upstairs. Jesse arrived for his usual visit and walked to the back of the building. When he saw me, he asked me why I was always outside. I tried to explain to him that we were just letting the children play together; it was nice to see Keithshon interacting with other children his age. That's when he grabbed me by the arm and told me not to talk back to him again. As far as I remember, that was the very first time I saw a different, uglier side of Jesse. After that, I stayed in the house when I knew he was coming over. I was determined to avoid any unnecessary confrontations.

Keithshon's second birthday was coming up and I really wanted to do something special just for him. This time was very important to me because I had never been able to do anything special for my son in the past. I was caught up in the excitement of his special day. Annie was kind enough to bake him a cake. I walked over to the Five Dollar Store to buy him some gifts, and then returned to sit outside and enjoy our time together. All of a sudden, feeling sick to my stomach, I ran into the bathroom to throw up. When I was done, I sat on the bathroom floor telling myself it was definitely time to leave this house. I knew I wasn't ready for another child, but it was true—I was pregnant again. Mrs. Henderson told me when I first arrived that I couldn't bring any more children into their home; there just wouldn't be enough room.

Jesse was extremely excited when I broke the news to him. He was happy about the prospect of us having a child of our own. Newly inspired, he spent the next two weeks diligently looking for a place to stay. We both understood the importance of us moving somewhere where no one could find us. I was a minor, still in the foster care system, and not free to just get up and leave without a big backlash. Even though I wanted to leave their home to have my own, I still wasn't ready to live alone with Jesse. Mrs. Henderson liked Jesse and he could never look bad in her eyes. Knowing she felt this way about him, I decided to keep the secret—Jesse was beating me. Despite this fact, I would still go live with him.

When we found a place to live, Mrs. Henderson promised that she would tell my caseworker that I had ran away and she had no idea where I had gone. Jesse had found a place in Korea Town off Wilshire Blvd. It was an old building with about 100 tenants. Our new apartment was a single. We didn't even have a mattress, so the owner provided the furniture. It was only Keithshon, Jesse, and I, so it would do for the time being.

Our first night in our new place, we sat on the floor and had Chinese food for dinner. Once we were done, we cleaned up our mess and decided to call it a night. Since we didn't have a radio or television, there was really nothing else for us to do, so we turned off the lights and went to bed. I woke up soon after because I felt something crawling on me. I tried to brush it off and go back to sleep, but over and over again this continued, until I got up and turned on the light. What I saw almost made me vomit and run screaming from the apartment. The entire wall and floor were covered with roaches! I had never seen anything like that in my life. A wall covered with nothing but these vile insects.

It was so bad! We grabbed the few things we had and left within minutes, deciding it would be best to get a motel room for the night. Jesse contacted the owner later and explained what we had experienced. The owner was very apologetic and promised to get on it right away. He immediately exterminated the apartment. It did not matter what he did, I was still extremely traumatized and refused to go back; but we did because we had nowhere else to go. After the apartment was fumigated, things were a little better, especially after I cleaned the place from top to bottom.

Every morning, Jesse left and was gone the entire day; sometimes he wouldn't come home at all. The only time he allowed me to go out of the house was when he let me ride with him to his mother's house. She still lived down the street from where my sister Christina lived, but Jesse had forbidden me to have any kind of relationship with my family. When we drove by my grandmother's house, I would have to duck all the way down in the car until we arrived at his parents' home. Now that he had me to himself, he had full control to treat me however he wanted, unrestrained. During the time that I was involved with Jesse, I got used to putting my head down, which made it easy for me to avoid accidentally glancing at someone while staring out the window and getting punched for doing so.

I learned the hard way not to glance at anyone after an "incident" that took place on the way to his mother's house. We were sitting at a signal, waiting for the light to change. A guy in a gold car pulled up next to us blasting his music. I looked over for a just a split second. Before I could turn my head and go back to staring straight ahead, Jesse lifted his right hand and slapped me across my face so hard that my head smashed up against the car door. Dazed and embarrassed, I nursed my lip, which had started to bleed profusely. Shocked at what he had just witnessed, the guy in the next car quickly recovered and stared ahead of him until he was able to drive off and remove himself from the awkward predicament.

Things with Jesse continued to deteriorate and he became increasingly dominant, to the point where I wasn't allowed to go outside at all. I couldn't even open the curtain in the house just to let the sun in;

and whenever Keithshon and I did go out, Jesse would find a reason to hit me. It was so bad that he would hit me and call me out of my name in front of his parents and siblings. His mom would try to say something whenever he would hit or scream at me, but she never seemed to convince me that she truly cared about what I was going through. He would tell her to shut up and mind her own business, and they would do just that, acting as if nothing had happened right in their presence. I was ashamed, sitting there on the couch sad and alone. They would just let me sit there, as though it was normal. This happened all the time. As time went on, Jesse stayed away from home a little longer each day. I was fine with that because I truly enjoyed my time alone with Keithshon. When I needed to talk to my sisters Eva and Christina, I would sneak to use the phone every now and again.

I was so tired of being pregnant, so I would find any and everything I could get into to help the baby come out faster. I would walk around the apartment, exercise, rearrange the furniture, I even ate different type of spices that were known to induce labor. Everything within reason that wouldn't hurt my unborn child! Just when I thought it would never happen, I went into labor. I was so happy because it would be an excuse for me to get out the house. This excitement didn't last long as Jesse proudly announced that he'd paid for me to have a midwife and have an at-home birth. This meant no hospital, people, or visitors. It was his way of making sure I wouldn't have a male doctor. He would always say, "I will never have another man looking at my stuff."

I told Jesse he should call the midwife to let her know that we were on our way to her home because it was time. It was three a.m. when he called and she was asleep. She got up and told us to come over. She lived about forty-five minutes away from where we stayed. She had a nice little house, and when we got there, she had a bedroom set up for me. When I was settled in, she took my blood pressure and pulse. After being there for a few hours, I really hadn't dilated much so I tried to get some rest. Jesse also slept in a chair in my room. Later on, he left to take care of "some business." The midwife told him it would be quite a while before I would deliver the baby. This was a very different experience for me. Of course, I had never given birth in a home before and didn't know what to expect. The midwife allowed me to eat Carl's Jr., which Jesse brought for me when he returned. I ate and she gave me some hot tea to drink. As I lay in the bed, I just kept thinking, *Wow, this is weird. How am I able to eat whatever I want and drink tea? I didn't get to eat anything when I was having Keithshon. All I was allowed to do was suck on ice chips.* When she came back in to check on me, I asked her would I be o.k. with the food I had just eaten. She smiled and said, "Yes, you don't have an I.V., so it's o.k. to eat and drink. You won't get sick."

For a full day, I just lay in the room alone until my little monster was ready to come out. When I finally went into full labor, the midwife took me to the toilet and had me wrap my arms around the back of it. After three pushes, I felt the pop and the baby's head was crowning. Jesse and the midwife carried me to the bed. Fifteen minutes later, a nine pound, ten ounce baby boy I named James was born. I nicknamed him Indian because he had the prettiest brown skin and jet-black hair that reminded me of a Native American doll.

Once we went home, things went back to normal. Jesse was always fussing and telling me what I was doing wrong, how I was neglecting the new baby for Keithshon, then leaving and staying away for days. I called my family, told them I'd had the baby, and that I would send a picture of him when I could. Keithshon was also very excited to have a baby brother because he now had someone else to play with. Unfortunately, Jesse made excuses as to why he didn't want Keithshon to hold his brother. He said he was too small and not to let him hold the baby yet because he might drop him. He would even get angry and make me feel bad when I would try to show Keithshon any attention. Keithshon was only two and he told me I was spoiling him. He would say "That's why he acts like a little b**ch!" I never said anything about it.

After a year, I was tired of sitting in the house. I wanted to go back to school. To make matters worse, I had no friends and missed my family. I had not seen them in two years. The last time I saw them was the day I'd left for the foster home. I knew Jesse wouldn't go for it. But after begging and pleading with him for months, to my surprise, he finally decided to let me enroll in school.

I started attending an adult school located near Washington Boulevard and the Interstate 10 freeway. I was very excited. I called four-one-one, got the information on a Tuesday, and went to the school to complete the application on Thursday. I started school the following Monday.

The first day of school, I woke up very early to feed the children and dress them. Even though the school I attended also provided childcare for young mothers, Jesse refused to let them come with me, so we would drop them off with the babysitter every morning. Jesse was afraid that I would take the children and leave him, so he always made sure we were separated. I don't know if I would have had the strength to do it if given the opportunity, but his fear may have become a reality.

I used to watch the other mothers playing with their children during the break, and wished I could do the same; I enjoyed just being around other people daily. My favorite part of school was free talk, a time scheduled for students to sit in a circle and share their issues about being teenage moms. Our teacher encouraged us and provided the support we desperately needed to deal with our issues. I kept to myself and did not speak a lot. My teacher saw something in me; she knew something was wrong. One day she told me that she knew I was involved in an abusive relationship because of the way I dressed and carried myself. When certain topics came up during our free talk discussions, I would get very tense. I didn't even realize I was reacting this way. Because my teacher was very familiar with the signs of a young woman who was being abused, she quickly spotted all of the signs in me. I was amazed that more than half of the girls there were in the same kind of relationship as me. I was even more shocked by the things I heard. One girl spoke about being dragged into the street by her husband after coming in late from her sister's house. No matter what, I would never share my story because I knew that if Jesse found out, he would beat me good, so I said nothing. Besides, I was only six months away from finishing school, and I was planning my next move.

One morning, I woke up and began my usual routine to get ready for school. Jesse told me that I couldn't go that day because he had things to do and didn't have time to drop me off or pick me up. I was so upset that I sat in the house all day crying, thinking to myself that if I put the children to bed early and went to sleep, the next morning would come quickly and I could go to school the next day. Jesse didn't come home that night. After that night, every day seemed to be like all the others. I would wake up and feed the children, put them in front of the television, sit on my favorite couch, and look out the window.

Jesse's brother, Ronald, would come by to visit the children and me on his lunch break. He and I were very close. He was the only one who wouldn't let Jesse talk badly to me or hit me. I enjoyed seeing him when he visited. Ronald worked around the corner from our apartment in an office building. He would call me to let me know that he was coming by for lunch, which he did a lot. I would always sit on the couch, looking out for him. We lived on the third floor, which meant that I could see him as soon as he arrived. He'd smile and wave, and I would wave back, running to the door to greet him.

Ronald always came bearing gifts for the children. We all enjoyed his company. We would laugh and crack jokes. He didn't have any children of his own, but he did have a stepson. Ronald brought gifts for every occasion—birthdays, Christmas, and just-because-I-love-you gifts. He also picked up the children and took them to the park, the zoo, and other places, which made my heart feel good. He was spending so much quality time with my children but I was never allowed to take them anywhere. Ronald would also go to bat for me when Jesse said the children couldn't go anywhere. Ronald was the eldest of the four children in the family, and even though Jesse didn't usually listen to anyone, he would listen to him, not arguing as much with Ronald as he did with other people.

After Jesse told me that I couldn't go back to school, I felt a change within me, a fundamental shift in my thinking. After that, I really didn't care about him hitting me or cursing me out the way I used to. I had finally decided that I wanted and deserved more out of my life. I started doing things I was normally too scared to do, and for the next few weeks, I didn't say very much to him. Deep down I felt numb, choosing to put all of my love and attention into my children.

I recall one day in particular. It started off pretty well. I was finally feeling like myself again, despite the beating I had taken from

Jesse a couple of days before. This time I got it just because the children were crying and wanted to go outside. I had taken them downstairs and let them play with some of the other children in the neighborhood. After being outside for about a half hour, Jesse approached me and told me to get in the house, which meant big trouble for me. For a moment, I thought I would be safe because his nine-year-old nephew was visiting. I assumed he would just let this one "offense" pass. I walked up the stairs slowly, hoping he would just leave once I went inside. That didn't happen.

As soon as I entered the apartment, he slapped me so hard that I fell to the floor, right in front of the boys. I was visibly shaken and afraid, and the children were as well, running to a corner of the room and crying hysterically. Jesse grabbed me by my shirt and pulled me up to choke me and knock me back down again. He then kicked me in my back, on my side, and in my stomach. I don't know what made him stop but he did. He left, taking his nephew with him. I was on the floor, unconscious. I don't even know how long I was out, but when I came to, the boys were sitting next to me, waiting for me to wake up. I crawled over to the phone and called Eva. I told her what happened, and asked her to please come and get the children and me.

It only took an hour before all my sisters pulled up to my house. Andrea had a bat, Christina had a gun; I don't know where she got it from. When they came in, two entered the room and two others stood at the door to watch for Jesse. They helped me grab the children and pack up whatever else I could carry on short notice. It was nice seeing my family again; they always came through for me when I needed them. I went to my aunt's house.

Seeing my family was as exciting as watching them with my children. Despite everything, my Aunt Bert never turned her back on me. Although she had shown me that tough love in the past, she welcomed me back home, which made me very emotional. She didn't really say much when I walked through the door, but I knew that she cared about me and missed me. Eva lived next door, so I had an opportunity to hang out with them as well, and they were able see James for the very first time. James was about eight months old and he was a big boy. They were all cooing over him and Keithshon, who was two years old by then. I was having so much fun with my family that I didn't want to go back home to Jesse.

One morning, I woke up and I wasn't feeling well; my stomach felt as if I ate some bad food the night before, so I made an appointment to see the doctor. After the examination, I learned that I was pregnant again. I just put my head down. I really didn't want to keep the baby, but I really wanted a little girl. I thought, *Maybe this could be my daughter!* I went back to my aunt's house and kept the news a secret.

I had been at my aunt's house for two weeks before Jesse found out I was there, and of course, he kept coming around. After realizing I couldn't stay with my family and have this baby because I knew there wouldn't be room for me and all my children, I decided to go back home. I figured that since he knew my family was back in my life that things would change. I was hoping that he would understand that he couldn't beat me anymore because now my family would protect me and take me away for good next time. So, equipped with a new resolve, I packed all my things and went back home. I kept quiet and stayed out of his way. For the rest of my pregnancy, I kept myself busy around the house and with the children. Jesse didn't come home much and I knew he was seeing someone else. At any rate, I didn't care as long as she kept him away from me. Life was good; I was so excited about the prospect of having a little girl.

One night God gave me a dream about the baby I was carrying and confirmed that it was a little girl! I was so happy. After that, nothing Jesse did seemed to bother me. I would just hug my stomach and ignore him. I began to sing to her, read to her, and dreamed of the day when I could dress her up, comb her hair, and put pretty barrettes in it. I could see myself getting her ears pierced and buying her cute little shoes. That was the happiest I had been in a very long time.

The big day finally arrived. It was truly one of the best days of my life—March 12, 1994, the day I went into labor with my daughter. I was happy because I was on my way to deliver at one of the most prestigious hospitals in Beverly Hills. It was a beautiful hospital, and I had my own radio and cable TV. I had never experienced this kind of luxury, so I was ready to relax and enjoy. I did just that whenever Jesse left to go take care of something. When he was there, it was bad because he argued with every male doctor who came into my room to try to check on me. He wouldn't even let them talk to me. He said it was bad enough that my regular doctor was a man, so all of these other men most certainly weren't going to be "all in my stuff."

Eventually, the hospital staff found a female doctor to come and check me until my doctor arrived. This wasn't the end of it. Once the pain got to be too much for me, the nurse came in to give me an epidural. Once again, Mr. Man showed out and got into it with the nurse. He told her that I couldn't have the shot; his reason was it could hurt the baby if they poked me in the wrong place. But this nurse was very determined not to let him bully her. She told him in his face that it wasn't up to him, and if I wanted the shot, it was up to me. If he tried to stop her, then she would have him escorted out, and that was that! I was in labor for eight hours with my daughter. She weighed five pounds, six ounces—a little bitty thing. I named her Jamie Ray. She was undoubtedly the prettiest little thing I had ever seen.

They wouldn't let me see her right away because I had a fever of one hundred three degrees, and they wanted to watch me closely. Once they put me in my room, I went right to sleep. I was so tired and sick that my body wouldn't allow me to stay awake until I could see her. When I woke up about an hour later, I was still unable to see Jamie. They told me that my fever was still high and that I needed to rest. As I lay in my bed, I realized that I hadn't had a chance to call my family, so I reached over, grabbed the phone, and called my sisters to tell them that I'd had a daughter. They were so excited! They asked what hospital was I in and what I needed. I explained that I hadn't had a chance to buy anything for her, so I pretty much needed everything. They told me that they were on their way out to pick up some things to bring up to the hospital for her. When Jesse found out I had called them, he was pissed. He made me call them back and tell them that they couldn't come and that we didn't need them to buy anything. He said that he was going to take care of his family and that he didn't need any help from them.

I was so upset. I cried hysterically, which didn't help my fever as it began to increase even more. My nurse came in the room and told him that he needed to leave to allow me to get some rest. I was in the hospital for the next three days. When I returned home with Jamie,

Jesse's family was waiting for us. I didn't really care for his mom because all she ever did was criticize my parenting skills. While they were all hovering over my new baby, I just sat in the corner alone, imagining myself in a different world—far, far away from them.

One year later, on March 21, 1995, I woke up feeling like a new person. I guess Jesse being gone for two days allowed me to feel like it was just me and the children, and we were a happy family; it was like a dream. Then the phone rang and I woke up from my dream. I already knew who it was, which was why I was hesitant to answer. When I did pick up the phone, he immediately started cursing and calling me out of my name. Because I didn't want to argue, I just said, "Whatever! I don't feel like hearing it!" and hung up. Jesse called me right back and told me that I was "in for it" when he got home. Terrified, I sat on the floor and stared into space. I was scared out of my mind. But I also knew that I couldn't continue living my life like this. I had to do something, if not for myself, I had to do it for my children.

That was the day that I told myself that I had finally had enough. I was not going to take any more of Jesse's abuse. Right then and there, I decided that if he came in fighting me then I was going to fight back with everything in me. It was around ten-thirty p.m. when Jesse got home. The children were already down for the night and I was sitting by the window in my chair waiting. Determined to make good on his promise, he rushed right in and came toward me, intent on hitting me. Before I knew it, I had jumped up on the chair, shouting for him to leave me alone and that he better not hit me anymore.

Fueled by his abusive temper, he just kept on coming toward me. That's when it happened. I reached down by my foot and picked up the big butcher knife I had placed there earlier. Before I could stop myself I swung it twice with all my strength. When I pulled it back, I glanced at the blade and noticed the blood on it.

Feeling the shock of the stabbing, he touched his head and fell backwards on the floor, unconscious. It was so surreal. All I could do was stand there and look at his still body, watching my short life suddenly flash right before my eyes. I started thinking I was going to go to prison for murder and my children would be placed in a foster home. Who would believe me? I had no proof of the abuse that I had suffered over and over again. Every time the police came out after one of my frantic nine-one-one calls, I would never follow through and file a police report against him. After about ten minutes of lying on the floor, Jesse came to, pulled himself up off the floor, and ran out of the house. After he left, I sat up all that night wondering what I was going to do. More importantly, I was worried about what he might do to me in retaliation. The next morning I packed whatever I could carry, grabbed the children, and walked the eleven blocks to my sister Christina's house.

Chapter Two:
How Could This Happen?

I stayed with Christina for about four months before I found my own place. It was a one-bedroom apartment right around the corner from Christina's house. I was so happy when the owner called me and said I'd gotten the place. It wouldn't be ready to move in for another two weeks but I was excited nonetheless. I was so proud of my determination to do better for myself and my children. This was the first apartment I had gotten on my own. I had long since stopped taking phone calls from Jesse and was reveling in my newfound independence. In a final attempt to win me back, he came over to my sister's house trying to entice me to give him another chance. He kept using that same old, tired line about how he would never hit me again. Jesse was getting so desperate, it was pathetic, but I knew the promises wouldn't last for long.

While visiting my grandmother who lived on 2nd Avenue and Arlington Boulevard, the very same block Jesse's mother lived on, I encountered Jesse as I was going to the store. It had been three weeks since I'd last seen him. I was walking to the store with my mom, and he suddenly pulled up in his truck and asked if we could talk. Disgusted, I refused to pay him any attention. Seizing his opportunity, he parked right in the middle of the street, jumped out, and followed behind us. He kept shouting at me, "Did you hear me?" At that time, my mother turned to him and demanded that he, "Get the hell on! She doesn't want to talk to you or have anything to do with your sorry a** anymore!" Now, why did she say that? It made him furious, of course!

At that point, he went for what he knew best and started insulting and cursing me. Then, to add insult to injury, he did the most humiliating thing a person can do to someone. Jesse told me I wasn't worth anything and was never going to amount to anything without him. He added that no one was going to want a woman with three children and then he spat right in my face. All I could do was stand there frozen in place, shocked beyond belief. As I thought about it, I wonder why I was so shocked after everything he had already put me through. I don't know, I can't even explain it, but I was. That's when my mom warned him that he'd better watch his back from that point on. Jesse had gone way too far and she wasn't going to let him get away with that. Jesse was a dead man!

Later that night, I replayed my entire relationship with him over and over in my mind. I sat up for very long time thinking, *How could I have been with someone so disrespectful for so long? Why and how had I allowed this man to tear me down and make me feel like the scum of the earth?* I went back to my earlier recollections of my childhood at Aunt Bert's, thinking about her and the rest of my family. I declared out loud, "I was raised better than that!" Although a bit dysfunctional, I came from a good family filled with strong black women who would beat a man down for looking at them sideways! My mother had taught us to pick up something and bash a person over the head with it if they even dared to look at us the wrong way, male or female! Believe me when I tell you, this was just to let them know not to ever try us again, not to even think about it. So tell me, how did I end up in the arms of this crazy man? I eventually fell asleep from all the back and forth conversation with myself.

The next morning at about seven a.m., I was startled out of my sleep by the phone ringing off the hook. Christina picked it up and I heard her talking loudly and excitedly, asking a lot of questions. At first, I couldn't tell who was on the phone. I later found out that my mom had been on the other end. I had the distinct impression that something bad had occurred. Christina was talking fast and sounded very anxious. "What happened? Where did it happen? Is he dead?" Finally, I heard her sigh with relief and say, "That's what his a** gets!" Curious, I got up and went to the bathroom quickly. When I came out, Christina came over to me and said that Mommy was on the phone. She had told her that Jesse had been shot. The shooting happened about three a.m. Evidently Jesse had been standing in the front yard of his mom's house. Someone had driven by, slowed down, and started shooting. Jesse was actually very blessed that he had only been shot in the buttocks. When the shooting started, he was able to run and duck down before he was seriously wounded. Nobody could prove that my mom was behind it, but everyone knew and left it alone.

I moved into my new place a few weeks later, and it felt like such a big accomplishment. It was certainly one of the better days. I didn't have much furniture but I made do with what I had. I gave the children the bedroom and I was happy to sleep in the living room. Although there were a lot of things that I needed to buy for my place to look and feel like a real home, I knew that I was blessed beyond measure to have what I possessed right then. I felt like this was the beginning of my new life and I cherished every minute of it. I was also ready to move up to the next phase in my life.

I enrolled in the School of Beauty and studied Cosmetology; before long, I had also found the children a childcare center. We were falling into a nice routine. Every day, I would wake up at six a.m., feed the children, dress them, and walk about eight blocks to the childcare center. After that, I walked another five blocks to catch my bus, arriving at school by eight-thirty a.m. In the evenings, I would leave school and repeat the same routine in reverse.

Once I got into the house, I would cook dinner, bathe the children, then put them to bed. Life was looking pretty good for us, and my family was just around the corner if I needed them. I became really good friends with one of my neighbors in the building, Cassandra. She lived on the floor just above mine and had three children of her own. We looked out for each other.

On December 5, 1995, we had just come home from spending an evening with friends. It was late, and the children were tired and hungry. I walked the children up the stairs, got them inside the house, turned on the light, and took off their jackets. I was holding Jamie and Indian was pulling at my pants with great determination, screaming, "Mommy, Mommy, I'm hungry." Keithshon was in the bedroom trying to put his things away. I became preoccupied with setting out pots to cook a quick dinner when I heard someone call my name from outside. I went to the window to see who it was and saw Cassandra standing by the gate. She was asking if someone could hold the gate open while she brought her groceries inside. I yelled down that I would come and do it. I told the children to sit down for a moment and that I would be right back. I walked down the stairs, opened the door, and stood there holding the gate open while she brought the groceries inside.

Cassandra lived on the third floor and I lived on the second. I was only outside for a few minutes when I heard someone yelling, "Fire!" Cassandra had come back downstairs and when I heard that word my heart dropped. We looked at each other and she screamed, "GO!" I could see my balcony from downstairs. The flames were coming from my apartment. I ran upstairs and had to pass through a door that led to our apartment. As soon as I opened the door, my heart plunged. I ran as fast as I could back through the doors that led to my apartment, but I couldn't see anything.

It was completely dark, with smoke filling the air. I rushed into the apartment, coughing and calling for my children by name. But I couldn't see anything. I started crawling on my hands and knees, feeling for their bodies. I could feel myself about to pass out, but I wasn't going to let that stop me. Fire was coming from the kitchen, and as I made my way there, I felt a body, grabbed it, and ran out of the door. I rushed down the hallway crying, and tried to give my son to the neighbors, but they wouldn't take him so I ran down the stairs. By that time, the fire department was pulling up.

Cassandra was standing at the gate and I gave her the child that I had. I looked at him and realized that it was Keithshon. I started running back to the apartment to find James and Jamie. By the time I got back through the door, I passed out.

When I woke up, I was downstairs on the ground. Afraid for my other two children, I tried to get up and go back to my apartment but Cassandra held me down and wouldn't let me get up. People were standing around and I could see the yellow tape. I was frantic, trying to get back into the apartment, yelling to anyone that would listen, "I've got to get my babies. I've got to get my babies!" Cassandra, clutching my arm, was trying her best to stop me from going back, but I was determined to get to my children. I pulled away from her and began running back toward the apartment. She pulled me back and tackled me to the ground. I couldn't understand why she wouldn't let me up to get to my children.

Cassandra continued to hold me down as I screamed helplessly and completely out of control by this time. Her strength, plus what she knew, wouldn't allow her to let me go. I looked past her and saw the reason why. Firemen were carrying James (burned over ninety percent of his body) and Jamie out on gurneys. They loaded them into the ambulance in front of the building. In a panic, I rushed after them and all I could see was more people standing around looking at me in disbelief. By then, my family had pulled up in their cars.

Christina's husband Marlon, who we called Moe, was an EMT. He had heard the call come over the radio and recognized the address. All of my sisters had arrived, rushing out of their vehicles and looking for me. When they saw me, one of them grabbed my hand, pulled me to the car, and we rushed over to the same hospital where I had given birth to Jamie. We parked and ran into the emergency room. Once inside, I checked in and they directed me to the location where my children were being examined. When I found them, they were lying next to each other, and I could hear them crying, "Mommy, Mommy, help me. It hurts . . . It hurts . . ." I went over to Jamie and just held her, but I couldn't hold her too tightly because she was in so much pain. I also tried to go over to Keithshon and hold his hand, but the doctor pulled me away and told me not to touch him. Dazed, it wasn't until I looked at him closely that I could tell that he was in excruciating pain.

The doctor then told me that I needed to be checked for smoke inhalation. Other medical staff came over to attend to me. I wouldn't allow them to touch me, but they kept repeating that I needed to be examined. One of them really pleaded with me to allow a doctor to examine me. I refused. I just couldn't fathom leaving my children in the state they were in to be examined myself.

As I was about to go back into the room with the children, I noticed police officers walking down the hallway. I paid them no mind as all my thoughts were consumed with worry about my children. The doctors would not allow me to come back into the room. They were prepping the children to go upstairs to undergo emergency surgery. I went over to the waiting room where all my family was gathered. After updating them on what was happening with the children, I sat down and sobbed, playing back the events of the evening over and over in my mind, wondering, *How did this happen? Why me? Why did this happen to my children?*

A little while later, I walked out into the hallway to get some air. Suddenly, a twisting pain of grief swept over me. I collapsed onto the floor, put my head into my hands, and wept uncontrollably. Once again, a nurse came over and pleaded with me to be examined for smoke inhalation. I was so caught up in my grief over my children that I begged him to leave me alone and just take care of the children.

When I was able to think rationally, I went to a pay phone to call Jesse, but his mother just cut me off and told me he wasn't home before I could tell her what had happened. Then she hung up the phone. My sister attempted to comfort me but I was inconsolable. At some point, the same two officers I had noticed earlier had come into the room asking to speak to me; one was a African-American male, short and slim, and the other was a stocky, Hispanic male. When I acknowledged them, they came over and asked if they could speak to me alone. I was reluctant, but there was no way out of speaking with them.

I was thinking that they simply needed to do the customary report about the fire. They took me into a small room and started asking me all of these questions. Because I was still in shock, I wasn't ready or able to answer their inquiries. Intent on getting me to talk, they insisted that I tell them how the fire got started and where I was at the time. They wanted to know why the children had been left alone, how long I'd left them, and where I'd gone when I left them alone. For several minutes, they kept grilling me and I still refused to answer. I even attempted to get up to leave the room to go check on my children. In an aggressive move to detain me, the African-American officer grabbed my arm and tried to stop me from leaving, but I caught him off guard when I used my body to push him away from me. Stumbling, the officer had to catch hold of a nearby table to break his fall. I took this opportunity to walk out of the door and head back to where my children were.

Catching up with me was relatively easy, the officer grabbed me and forced my hands behind my back and told me I was under arrest. Too caught up in my need to see my babies and still suffering from the residual effects of all the smoke I had inhaled trying to rescue them, I still tried to get away. I didn't understand why they were doing this to me when my children were there fighting for their lives. As they marched me down the hallway past my family, they stopped long enough to advise them that I was being taken down to the station for questioning.

My sisters cried out in protest and burst into tears. As I was being escorted out to the squad car, Jesse's brother Garry was walking toward the hospital. I wanted to ask if Jesse was on his way to the hospital, but the look on his face said it all. Apparently, Garry blamed me for this tragic turn of events. He looked at me with hatred in his eyes. It was as if I could read his mind and hear him saying, "How could you let this happen? You deserve everything that's coming your way." At the moment, I could do nothing but put my head down and let the tears roll down my face.

When I arrived at the police station, the officers asked the same questions they had asked at the hospital over and over again. "Why did I leave the children in the house? Where did I go? How long was I gone? Did I lock the door to the apartment intentionally?" By the time they were finished questioning me, I was so tired. I just wanted to go back to the hospital. When I asked how much longer it would be, they informed me that I wasn't going to leave, and they were charging me with child endangerment. At that moment, my whole body went limp.

They told me that I could make a phone call if I wanted to. The only person I wanted to talk to was my aunt. She answered on the first ring and said she had been waiting for me to call. I told her that they were arresting me, but she said she already knew because it was all over the news. After she told me this, my mind was racing. I didn't have a clue how my life been turned upside down like this. They took me to a holding station in downtown Los Angeles; I repeatedly ask if I could make a phone call, but the officer at the front desk kept ignoring me.

The television was on and the story of the fire was all over the news. There was a female officer on duty who was watching the newscast and she kept looking at me with disgust. I was finally moved to a cell with a phone in it. I called Jesse. He was at UCLA Harbor Hospital sitting with Indian, and he actually asked me if I was okay. I admitted to being afraid and asked him to keep an eye on the children until I could get back to them. He told me he had been talking to mutual friends of ours that knew my family and they had informed him it wasn't looking good for me. I told him that I would call him back to check on them to see what was going on.

I was moved to a cell with eight bunks. All the bunks were being used except for one of the top bunks, so I assumed that would be my bed for the night. I couldn't fall asleep because one cellmate, a white, heavy-set woman, kept staring at me. She kept getting up to use the toilet, and would sit there and stare at me without saying a word. I wondered if she was crazy or if she knew my story and was passing the same judgments on me as the guard had as she'd watched the newscast. I turned away from her, faced the wall, and slept. My sisters Yolanda and Angie brought me some clothes. I was still wearing the same clothes that smelled of smoke, a gray Mickey Mouse sweatshirt, jeans, and tennis shoes.

The officers allowed me to change my clothes and talk to my sisters. They told me that they were trying to get an attorney for me. My sisters had called a press conference in front of the apartment building. They wanted to dispel all the lies that were flying around about the circumstances of the fire. At the press conference, all my sisters were there and pleading for justice on my behalf. There were people who didn't even know me, giving false statements to the reporters. According to them, I had left the children in the house to go out and smoke drugs, or I was out partying so I locked them in the house to make sure they couldn't leave. I couldn't believe the stories I was hearing! People will say anything for fifteen minutes of fame. They all wanted time in front of the camera in my opinion. All of this just gave the police more reasons to hold me longer.

My big break came when a Hispanic man whom I had never met told reporters that even though he didn't really know me, he did know that I was a good person and a great mom because I had shown a lot of love and kindness to his daughter Maria. One day, this little girl was outside playing with my children on a cold afternoon without a coat or sweater on. I took off my son's jacket, put it on her, and never asked for it back. He was already quite warm, having multiple layers of clothes on. After hearing that story and talking to my family and friends, they decided to release me.

I was in jail for about a week before I was released. One of the officers had already given me the heads up as I was being processed out. Still, I was not prepared for the media frenzy waiting for me. When I appeared, reporters came flying out of nowhere within seconds. They were relentless, asking some of the most intrusive questions I have ever heard! I couldn't deal with it so I sat inside the station until my family came to pick me up. It was a couple of hours before we were able to leave. As soon as my sisters pulled up, they were forced to talk to reporter after reporter. We were finally able to escape, but not for long.

When we arrived at my aunt's house, they were there, too. We gave them the slip and went in through the back door. My sister Andrea went outside to demand that they leave and give me some peace. I couldn't sleep at all that night, thinking constantly about my children and wondering how soon I could go see them at the hospital. First thing the next morning, I got up, took a shower, and headed to the hospital to visit them. I checked in at the front desk and was told that they were in ICU on the fourth floor. When I got off the elevator, I walked over to the nurse in charge to ask where they were located. Before I could utter even one word, she gushed, "We were waiting for you!" and proceeded to take me to my babies. When I walked in, I just stood there staring in amazement. There were stuffed animals everywhere! She then explained that people had been dropping off all kinds of gifts for days. When I finally saw the children, they were lying in two beds right next to each other. They were heavily sedated because they were in constant pain. Wracked with guilt, I burst into tears and went over to them. I stayed for about an hour then headed over to USC Medical Center to check on Indian. He had been moved there for better care.

This would be the first time I had seen James since the fire. He was the one who had been burned the worst. He was also in ICU, so I was required to wash my hands, and put on a gown and mask before entering his room where he was in isolation. As I walked into the room, I noticed he was wrapped in bandages and gauze from head to toe. He had already undergone two surgeries to treat his extensive burns. Gasping, I held back my tears because I didn't want to scare him. Carefully, I took his hand and tried to get him to respond to my touch but he too was heavily sedated for the pain. The nurse told me that he had been this way since he was brought in.

I sat with him until around eight that evening. Exhausted, I finally went home to try to get some sleep in order to be rested for the dark days ahead. The next morning I arrived at the hospital early because Keithshon and Jamie were being transferred to private rooms, and I wanted to make sure I was there when they woke up. Jamie was doing a little better, but she wouldn't speak and always kept her head down. Even though she was only one and a half, I knew she understood something tragic had happened. I remember trying to take her into the bathroom to wash her face. When I put her in front of the mirror, she turned her head away and wouldn't look at herself. With my heart in my throat, I took her back to her bed, gave her the biggest hug I could manage, and stayed with her until she fell asleep. After that, I went across the hall to Keithshon's room to give him a bath. I then sat with him for a couple of hours until visiting hours were over. It was now time to go over to UCLA to be with Indian. After spending most of the night with him, I went home to rest for a little while.

Early the next morning, I prepared myself to do the same thing all over again. Gathering the strength that I needed to face my reality, I took a shower and headed back to the hospital for Jamie's seven a.m. physical therapy session. That routine would be my life for the next few weeks. Keithshon was the first to go home. He was sent to live with my sister Christina because the courts ruled that I was unfit to take care of him. Although that was painful, I couldn't take my focus off my goal, which was to make sure that they all were okay. Actually, that decision was an immense blessing because it was much easier to have just Jamie to watch over. It also allowed me more time to spend with Indian, and given his circumstance, every second counted.

It was a Thursday evening and I had just gotten home from UCLA Medical Center. Indian's doctor called to let me know they needed my permission to move him over to CHOC (Children's Hospital of Orange County). He had taken a turn for the worse and his breathing had started to fail. In order to save him, they needed to fly him over there right away. I paused before saying anything, giving myself a few seconds to process this unsettling news. He had been at UCLA for three weeks and I thought for sure he was getting better. After snapping back to reality, I gave them the okay, then headed out to meet them.

When I got to CHOC, they already had him hooked up to the artificial lung machine to help him breathe. When I got there, I rushed to his room and sat with him all night, falling asleep by his side. The next morning, a nurse came over to me and asked if I lived in the area. I told her, "No, I live in Los Angeles." As if waiting for her cue, she told me about the Ronald McDonald House and said she would handle the paperwork to get me immediate access to lodging. True to her word, later that evening she made all the arrangements for me to stay there during Indian's hospital stay. This made it much easier for me to stay in town, instead of asking for rides or taking the long bus ride back and forth between Los Angeles and Orange County. Everything had been taken care of by the time I arrived at the Ronald McDonald House. I knew how scary this whole ordeal was for my Indian and I wanted to be there right by his side. That night, I stayed up with him all night and left early in the morning to get Jamie ready to be discharged.

After Jamie was discharged, I spent that day with her and Keithshon, then I went back to the Ronald MacDonald House. I left RMH on Christmas Eve; I wanted to be with Keithshon and Jamie on Christmas Day to try to make sure they had a good Christmas despite everything that had happened.

Christmas Day was spent at my aunt's house with my family. Christina brought Keithshon, Angie brought Jamie, and I spent the night with them. Several people had very generously donated toys when they heard about the fire. My friend Mickey called a local radio station and told them my story. I won the Secret Santa gift and representatives from the station dropped off toys to my aunt's house. That was a nice surprise and a welcomed distraction from all that was going on.

I stayed with Indian day in and day out. I brought a lot of clothes with me since I was so far away and wasn't able to go back and forth.

I really didn't care about being there around the clock. Indian needed me and I needed to be with him. I didn't really eat much during that awful time. All I could do was get up in the morning, go sit with him, and hope he would wake up for just a moment. I would pray for him to open up his eyes for even a few quick seconds.

I got up early one Thursday morning and decided to hang around the Ronald McDonald House to fix myself a nice breakfast and catch up on some rest. I received a call from Dr. Humphrey, who wasted no time asking me to attend an important meeting. Once I got there, I saw that Jesse and his mother were already in one of the conference rooms waiting for me. I didn't know what to expect because they had never made any attempts to visit Indian while I was there. I just grabbed a seat to listen to what the doctor had to say. Jesse's mother and I were careful not to make eye contact with each other. I didn't feel like the petty rolling of the eyes from her. It had already been made clear by his whole family that it was my fault my children where in this situation. Getting straight to the point, the doctor started explaining why he thought we should take Indian off life support.

Earlier in the day, the medical team had taken him off the machine to see if he could breathe on his own, but within a minute or so his heart rate had started to drop. He proceeded to inform us that Indian wouldn't be able to live without being hooked up to the breathing machine at all times. He maintained that it would be easier for everyone involved to take him off the machine. While I sat there in silence, Jesse and his mother started to argue with the doctor. They told him that he wasn't going to kill their son/grandson. They even started to get up in his face in an aggressive manner.

As I sat and watched these two do what they did best—make complete fools of themselves—I was fed up. I said to myself, "I can't take this anymore!" I got up and walked out. Before the doctor exited the room behind me, I heard him tell Jesse and his mother to either calm down or leave the premises. As he passed me, he stopped long enough to say that he was sorry that I had to go through this ordeal and wished me the best.

I went back into the room where Indian was sleeping, and sat there holding his hand. Bowing my head, I said a prayer and asked the Lord if it was His will to take him, then please do it quickly. I was sad and tired of being sad, and I really didn't want to be the one to make that very final decision. Around eight p.m., a nurse came in the room and asked me to step outside for a second. They needed to check his vitals and chart his progress. I took this opportunity to stretch my legs and get a snack downstairs. When I returned, the doctor pulled me aside and told me that he was sorry to inform me that Indian had passed away about seven-forty-five pm. Feeling my world crashing around me, I fell to my knees and sobbed until a nurse came over and helped me to my feet. That day will be forever frozen in my mind. It was January 14, 1996. Taking a few more minutes to compose myself, I called my family to let them know that I needed someone to come to the hospital as soon as possible to be with me.

About an hour later, I was sitting in a private room with Jesse and all my sisters waiting for the coroner to come and take my baby's body away. Grief-stricken, I sat holding him in my arms, rocking him as if he were asleep. As I rocked back and forth, I sang to him for the last time and told him how much I loved him and was going to miss seeing his face every day. Jesse was standing by my side, trying to stop crying. He had just taken Indian out of my arms to say his goodbyes when the coroner came in. He asked in a respectful manner if we were ready, and as I gave my child one last kiss, I told him yes. He placed him down gently on the bed and took out a tag that had all his information on it, placing it around his leg. He placed the body bag on the table and put my Indian's tiny body inside it, closing it slowly. As I looked around the room, all I could see were tears. Then he put him on the gurney and we all followed him out of the room down to his hearse outside, and watching closely in despair as he placed Indian in the front seat, fastening his seat belt as if he were going on his last ride home to heaven. I stood and watched the car pull away until I couldn't see it any longer.

After arriving at my aunt's house from the hospital, I didn't want to be around anyone so I went and sat on the front porch. Eva came outside where I was sitting in the dark, quiet corner, and scooted next to me; we sat in silence for a long time. We didn't look at each other, but she put her arms around me and we cried together. She rubbed my back and held me until I finally went back into the house. I sat in a quiet place until everyone left. I went to lie down on the couch soon after, but didn't sleep at all that night. As I was sitting on the couch alone in the dark, I thought about everything that had happened since the fire.

I woke up several times during the night and finally fell into a deep sleep around six-thirty a.m. the next morning. I woke up around ten a.m., and I felt like my heart was broken in a million pieces. The pain was beyond description. I was sitting there thinking that I needed to do something very drastic. I needed another source of pain to take away the searing pain I was feeling every waking moment. That's when I decided that I wanted to get a tattoo.

Around ten-thirty, I abandoned the thought of going back to sleep so I caught the bus to a tattoo parlor. I didn't really know exactly what I wanted, but I knew that I needed something to take the pain away. After sitting for two hours, I finally drew a picture of Indian with angel wings and "R.I.P." under the drawing, and got it inked on the back of my shoulder. When I got back home, my family told me that they had been extremely worried about me. My sisters wanted to check on me to make sure I was okay. All I really wanted was to be left alone. Feeling the need to escape for a while, I went and sat on the floor in the corner behind the couch until I fell asleep.

People started coming by the next day. Everybody came to pay their respects and generally wanted to see how I was doing, and to find out when the funeral was going to be. Before my family and I could make the funeral arrangements, I received a phone call from Jesse's mom who told me that they were already taking care of everything. I was okay with all of this at first, until we called the mortuary to reserve a car for our family, and we were told that the father's family had instructed them not to give us a car. There was to be only one car reserved for their family and the funeral was going to take place a week later. They wanted to wait for Jesse's older brother Ronald to return from a business trip, especially since he was paying for everything.

Jesse and his family had taken the position that if they were paying for everything, they didn't have to give us anything. I got so pissed off that I informed the funeral home's representative that I was the child's mother and wouldn't allow the body to be released to them, so they could just cancel everything. I couldn't understand why his family would do what they had done, until I got a phone call from

Ronald. At first, I was very happy to hear from him because he was the only one I was close to in that family and he understood me. My happiness faded when he started cursing me out, telling me that it was my fault and that I had killed my son. He told me that if I had stayed with Jesse and kept my family together, none of this would have happened.

At that moment, I blacked out. I started yelling and going off. I threw the phone at the wall and ran out of the house barefoot. I had no idea where I was going. I vaguely remember running into an intersection, and just as suddenly as I started running, I stopped and started to walk very slowly. I saw the car coming faster and faster, but I didn't care. I couldn't stop! I didn't want to stop! I told myself that everything would be okay very soon. I had stepped off the curb, confident that everything would be okay no matter what occurred. I walked into traffic never looking to the left or right; I kept my eyes straight and kept walking, waiting for it to all be over. Yet, the impact I had braced myself for never came. The car swerved and I heard a loud honk, but I didn't care. I just kept walking until I realized I was on the other side of the street. Looking back, I couldn't understand how I made it across untouched. Still in a haze, I didn't even try to figure it out. I just kept walking, and when I did look up, I realized that I was at Christina's house.

She'd moved out of the back of my grandmother house into a large two-bedroom apartment just a few blocks from my aunt's house a few years earlier. Keithshon was staying there and I hadn't planned to go see him. Actually, I really didn't want to see anyone; but as I was walking up the steps to her apartment, I knew God had sent me to him. I went into the house and he was sitting on the floor watching television. I gathered him into my arms and held him tightly—never wanting to let go.

The day of the funeral finally arrived. I was ready for all of this to be over. I was so tired of the fighting and stress between the two families. Since I didn't let Jesse's family pay for it, they decided they were going to let me suffer and handle everything on my own, fully aware that I didn't have any money. But God had better plans because my own family came to the rescue, pulling together every available resource that was needed for my Indian.

Everyone met at my aunt's house and we got dressed there. We had two limos for the family. I was the last to get dressed, and an instructor from the Cosmetology school on Crenshaw and 43rd did my hair. I was silent on the drive over to the mortuary, mainly staring out the window into space. My silence set the tone. No one with me spoke either; they just watched me out of concern. I'm sure they were worried about how I would react at the service. I believe they thought that I might lose it at any moment, because I hadn't cried for days. I had already wept so much that I had given in to the grief. There were no tears left.

I was in a daze for much of the service. My sister was holding Jamie and one of my cousins was taking care of Keithshon. Everyone was watching me, but I didn't move or make a sound until it was time for me to walk up to the casket and say my final farewell to my baby boy. That's when I lost it. The composure I'd held onto for the last few days fell away, and I was lost in a world of pain, weeping inconsolably for my dead child.

When the service ended, we were all getting ready to leave when a mortuary assistant stood up and said he had an announcement. He then stated there was a change of plans with regard to the burial. Indian was no longer to be cremated, and that we should all follow the hearse over to Inglewood Cemetery for a proper burial. Confused by what had just taken place, l was informed that a famous rapper had seen the story on the news and volunteered to pay for a proper burial.

I'm not sure how but Calvin Broadus, who is professionally known as Snoop Dogg, heard about the fire and Indian's death. He very generously offered to pay the expenses for the funeral and burial. He personally went over to the cemetery and took care of everything. The amazing part of the whole event wasn't that he took the time to go to the funeral home himself, but the fact that he decided to perform this random act of kindness and generosity in the midst of his own murder trial. Snoop stopped by the mortuary on the day of the funeral before we arrived to see how the family was doing. He didn't want to meet us; he explained that he didn't want to take away from the family mourning the child. His trial was the same day as the funeral, yet he had taken the time to pay his respects before meeting with his attorney. He was adamant about staying anonymous. He never talked about it during media interviews, and it never came up in articles about him. He didn't discuss it all.

Years later, I would have the opportunity to meet him while I was working on his movie *Da Game of Life*. I finally had the opportunity to introduce myself. I was sitting in his dressing room with some other people, and when he came in, I went over to him and introduced myself as the mother of the child who had perished in the fire back in '96. As I spoke to him, tears were flowing down his cheeks. He exhibited a kind heart and so much compassion. I really didn't think he would remember because it had been such a long time. He was just amazed that I was sitting there with him. I'll never forget the emotion of that meeting with him.

During the ride over to the cemetery, the traffic was absolutely crazy. There were so many cars that some of the cars had to get out of the line just to block traffic. When we were turning a corner, one of my sisters told me to look out the window to see just how many people had come out to show their love. For the first time in a long time, I smiled a little.

It had been a week since the funeral; all I wanted to do was sit in the room with the door closed and lie on my bed. I was glad that I was home with my aunt again. One day, she came home, pushed open the bedroom door, and told me that I was not going to be able to stay with her forever. It was time to get up off my butt and get a job so I could find my own place. She saw me going into a deep depression and thought I would try to do something crazy again. She had found out about my walk into oncoming traffic before the funeral. She was forcing me out of the hole I was falling into. As I'd lain in the bed with my children, I wanted to act as if my world was in the confines of those four walls. The last thing on my mind was getting a job. I was not ready to go out into the world just yet, but my aunt wasn't giving up on me. She was a very strong woman and had raised us all to be the same way. At first, I thought she was being cold hearted, but she was just doing what she knew, giving me tough love.

Every day I would look for a job but I never really put much effort into it. I was soon hired at a store called The Price Club. I hated that job! The employees recognized me from the news, so whenever I was in the lunchroom people would just stare and point. Finally, I just stopped going in there all together. The restroom became my favorite place in the whole store. I even went there when I should have been working. It got to the point that whenever my supervisor would look for me, she would tell a co-worker to go to the restroom and tell me they needed help on the floor. I realized I didn't want to work there and started to look for another job.

I saw a phone number for "Braids by Katrina" in a local newspaper and called. I spoke with the owner who explained that the shop would be open in two weeks, and she still had two stations to fill. She told me the available work hours, and the pay would be split sixty-forty-sixty percent to me and forty percent to her. Everything sounded good to me, so we set up a time for me to come in the next day to show her my braiding skills. It took only five minutes for her to tell me I was hired and she gave me a "Braids by Katrina" T-shirt.

I started work the same day the shop opened, April 14, 1996, and I arrived bright and early. I thought I would be braiding hair that morning, but instead she had me pass out flyers. The shop was really far from my house, and I still didn't have a car, so I had to take the bus. Sometimes I would get off very late at night when the buses had stopped running. On those days, I slept in the shop.

Seven months later, I was finally ready to try to move out of my aunt's house into an apartment of my own. I was making good money at the shop. The owner and I had become very good friends. I really looked up to her. She was twenty-five years old with two children and had her own successful business. This girl could take an idea and turn it into anything! I was just amazed. Some nights, when she worked late, she would take me home even though it was out of her way. I mean, don't get me wrong, we bumped heads a lot, but she had a good heart. She was also one of the reasons I started dating again. She told me it was time to put the past behind me, that I was a pretty girl, and I shouldn't be afraid to live my life and trust again. I decided she was right. It was time for me to let someone into my life again. I decided to be a bit more open about dating but I didn't want anything to take my mind off making more money so I could get my own place.

One particularly busy day in the shop, the owner was braiding this very interesting woman's hair. Everyone in the shop couldn't quite believe how she was dressed and how she talked. I wasn't tripping about her or her appearance. Besides, who was I to judge anyone? I had a mother who had been on drugs most of my life and I had been through enough to know that you should never judge a book by its cover. There is always something good hiding beneath the surface.

Now, I will say that she had a very bad mouth. She talked freely about having sex with guys and how she made them pay for it. She also told us that she was a dancer and how she could make a few thousand dollars a week. She then looked over at me and said, "Hey have you ever thought about dancing? You are a very pretty girl with a nice body, and if you ever want to make some real money, you should think about working at my club. You could definitely be one of the top moneymakers. Initially, I acted like I knew all about strip clubs, but in reality, I had never been in such a club or even met a stripper before in my twenty years of life.

That day after work, I was standing at the bus stop when the woman from the shop drove up and asked if I wanted a ride home. My first instinct was to say, "No, thank you," but I was tired and gladly accepted her offer. She told me her name was China. As she drove fast with her music up as loud as it could go, I didn't really know what to talk about with her. From her talk in the shop, she seemed to have a lot of life experience. What kind of conversation could I offer? She was everything that I wasn't—confident, independent, and worldly.

The ride on the way home was very quiet, except for the music. When we pulled up to my house, she told me about a club that I should check out. She added that I was supposed to be twenty-one to work there, but they wouldn't care about my age because of the way I looked. She told me that when I actually turned twenty-one, she would bring me into her club to work. I sat up all night thinking about what China had told me. I rationalized that since I was trying to get my own place, it wouldn't be a bad idea to go check it out; the extra money would help a lot. I mean, what harm could that do—right?

Chapter Three:
Who's that Girl?

My first night walking into a club, I wasn't as nervous as I thought I would be—until it was time for me to go up on stage. David's was a little hole in the wall where the neighborhood guys would hang out, and they spent a lot of money. My first time on stage, I froze. I couldn't seem to move until this guy came, sat right in front of the stage, pulled out some money, and dropped it down on the stage. I came a little closer and started to dance a little to the music. By the second song, there were about five guys standing around, watching and tipping really big. Seeing their response to me made me really get into it. It may sound strange, but they actually made me feel more comfortable about being up there. It was as if I was receiving encouragement and support. I was being welcomed and given their stand of approval. After I finished dancing and left the stage, there were a few guys waiting for me to give them a lap dance. I discovered that was where I would make the real money.

I remember this one guy sitting in the corner staring at me the whole time I was on stage. As I was coming off the stage, he grabbed me and said he was first in line for a private dance. As I started to dance for him, he asked my name; I told him that I hadn't come up with one yet. He immediately suggested I call myself Fantasy because, "You are definitely mine." From that moment on, that was my name. I stayed at David's until I turned twenty-one.

I was now old enough to work at China's club. The first time I stepped into The Players Spot was a Wednesday night. I went to participate in their amateur night. China Doll was already there waiting for me to arrive. When I saw her, I felt at ease. This club was very different from David's. It was bigger and had more girls who were prettier and had nicer bodies. The Players Spot was fancier. The girls wore garters around their thighs to hold all the money they made, and they made a lot! Men surrounded the stage and threw large sums of money at the two girls who were on stage when I arrived. I felt as if I were in another world, I had never seen anything like this except in rap videos. Before I went on stage, China Doll took me to the dressing room and introduced me to some of the girls. Even though some of them didn't want to speak, they did anyway because they all had respect for her.

China helped me pick out an outfit for the stage and told me all the do's and don'ts of dancing at The Players Spot. She also let me know that she had invited some of her customers to tip and vote for me so I could win; girls who won amateur night were hired. As I sat outside the dressing room watching all the girls step on and off the stage, I couldn't believe how much money these girls were making. As soon as they put their money away, they would have to run and do lap dances until it was time to go back on stage. Seeing all the money and the caliber of the girls who worked there, all I could think to myself was, *I am so ready to work here!*

The amateur contest was about to start and I was suddenly nervous. I didn't think I would be able to perform. I took a sip of a drink and reminded myself that I needed to make this money to get a place for me and my children. I took a deep breath, walked up the stairs, went behind the curtain and came out on stage when my name was called.

I was really happy when I finally finished dancing. I was even happier to learn that I had won.

As I was changing back into my clothes in the dressing room, the manager of the club asked me to come into his office. He offered me a job and asked when I could start. He said there was a guy outside who wanted to get a couple of lap dances from me. I tried to tell him that I would come in one day the following week, but he suggested I should go out on the floor and do a few dances before I left. There were some high rollers who had requested me. He said I shouldn't pass up such an opportunity. Taking a deep breath, I closed my eyes and said a prayer. I can't say exactly why I prayed—I wasn't a spiritual person in those days—but for some reason I felt that I needed to do it before I went out on the stage. I went home with a nice amount of money in my purse. This was my new reality and I gladly accepted it.

I was making really good money at my new club. I was able to move into a one-bedroom apartment and buy all new furniture. I was even able to buy my first new car. It wasn't much but it was mine. Working at The Players Spot and making all the money I was making, allowed me to handle my financial obligations finally.

I told myself that I was only going to dance for a few years to save up money to buy a house, pay off all my bills, and put away money for my children's future. Before I could fully move forward with my plans, I need to clear up some issues that still lingered from the fire that had claimed Indian's life and scarred Keithshon and Jamie. My first obligation was to pay off all my court-mandated parenting class fees and obtain my parenting certificate. This showed the court that I had taken the necessary steps to regain custody of my children. This was my most pressing concern and it felt great when I got them back.

Everything was going well, my children were home where they belonged, and I'd met a great guy named Shawn Gamble. Shawn and I were going strong by then. It had been five months since we'd met, but our relationship was already pretty intense. I can remember like it was yesterday. He was tall, dark, and handsome. He had the ability to make me laugh, and we enjoyed each other's company a great deal.

The only problem with Mr. Gamble was that he was a true ladies' man, and he wasn't shy about letting that little fact be known. In the beginning, I thought I could deal with it. As time went by, I realized that I wasn't as into an "open relationship" as I thought.

In spite of my best arguments with myself, I started to fall for him and couldn't walk away. I guess it was my love for bad boys that kept me interested enough to stay. No matter what he did when I wasn't around, he took care of me as if I was his only girl. He made sure that he dropped me off at work and picked me up before I purchased my car. If he had plans with anyone else, he would change them just to make sure he was always there for me but, of course, when he was out with other girls I would call him just to see if he would pick up and he always did.

Living around the corner from my family enabled me to receive a lot of help from them. They helped out as much as they could, and even watched the children while I went to work. Jesse really didn't do much for Jamie, so I never bothered to ask him for anything. Truth be told, I never expected anything anyway.

Shawn tried to help me as much as I would allow him to. I had really started to fall hard for him. It didn't help that my family loved him as much as I did, that was just the way it was with Shawn; he had a way with people, especially people of the opposite sex. I seriously thought I was the luckiest woman in the place whenever I went out with him. Women would stop in their tracks when they saw him. He was tall with light brown eyes, always dressed nice, and he constantly wore his winning smile. It wasn't always easy being with him. Although I never really had to worry about the younger girls flirting with him, it was always the women who were ten to fifteen years my senior who would step on my toes. They'd do anything to get his attention.

One Friday night, my cousin Sheila had a birthday party at a club in Century City. As usual Shawn and I were dressed to impress and ready to party. Everyone was happy to see us out together. They already knew we were all going to dance, laugh, and have a good time when Mr. Gamble was in the house.

That night at Shelia's party, I was on the dance floor with my family, laughing and having fun, until I suddenly realized that I hadn't seen

Shawn in a while. I walked around the club looking for him. Of course, he was at the bar with a bunch of women standing around him trying to get his attention. I walked over and told him that we would be leaving in a while, advising him not to disappear. One of these women evidently thought that I was just some girl trying to get his attention, because she walked around him, stood right in front of me, and started engaging him in conversation. Now, my first thought was to pick up my glass and break it across her head, but I remembered that I was with my family, and if I started a fight, my family would no doubt jump in. Plus, I didn't want to ruin the party so I decided to walk away.

A few minutes later, Shawn came over to where I was standing on the dance floor. Being his charming self, he took me by my waist, pulled me close to him, and told me to stop tripping. By that point, I was too mad to let the incident pass. Just as I was about to walk away and let Shawn think about his action, the same woman from the bar brought him a drink. He laughed and thanked her. I immediately turned and walked away from him, leaving him standing there alone. He kept dancing alone until Sheila, the birthday girl, made her way over to him and asked what was wrong. He replied, "Oh, she's mad because some woman bought me a drink." Finding it quite funny, they laughed and laughed. He slept on the floor that night, but the relationship continued.

A few weeks later, Shawn was supposed to come over to my house to help me set up my new entertainment center. When he called to say he was on his way, he mentioned that he had to make a quick stop first. After waiting for over two hours for him to arrive, I began to worry. I called him several times and left messages. He didn't return any of my calls. Around six-thirty that evening, his brother called me and told me that Shawn and their cousin had been arrested.

Apparently, his cousin had been caught with stolen stereo equipment in the vehicle, and Shawn was with him, so they both were arrested. His brother said that Shawn was going to try to call me as soon as he got the chance. In that moment, my heart dropped and I couldn't think or speak. I sat on my couch and stared at the television for about an hour. Shawn wasn't able to call me until about eight that night. Although I was worried and concerned, I was extremely happy to hear his voice on the line. He explained how everything had happened and told me that things weren't looking good, but not to worry. He promised to call me as soon as he found out what he was facing. He called me every day for the next two weeks while he waited for his court date.

When Shawn's court date arrived, I wanted to be there for him. I didn't have anyone to watch the children, so I had to wait for his brother to call me to tell me what happened. That entire day I tried to keep myself busy by cleaning up my house and running errands. Anything I could do to distract myself from my anxiety. When my phone rang, I dropped everything and ran to pick it up. When I answered, his brother immediately asked me if I was sitting down. Before he could say anything else, I bombarded him with questions. "Did you see him? How did he look? What did they say? Is he alright?" I paused to ask my next question, and he was able to break in and tell me that Shawn was fine.

Shawn's lawyer couldn't do much since they were caught red-handed. He was sentenced to two years in jail. The news was devastating. I didn't know what I was going to do! I had never been in a situation like this before. When Shawn was finally able to call, I told him that I had decided to stand by him and wait for him while he was doing his time.

I didn't think waiting would really be that hard. I thought with work and the children that the time would just fly by. Over the next couple of months, I stayed really busy. I managed to change my work schedule so I could visit Shawn on the weekend. He was incarcerated at a facility five hours away from Los Angeles. I had to get up at three-thirty in the morning to check in at eight a.m. Waking up at three-thirty a.m. on the weekend to visit him was hard, but seeing him made it all worth it. I would light up like a Christmas tree when he entered the visiting room.

Four months passed and the situation wasn't getting any easier for either of us. During those four months, Shawn had been moved four times, been on lock down, and denied phone privileges because of a riot. We talked on the phone as often as possible despite all this. During one of our phone calls, he told me that he really loved me. He had been thinking about his life and where he wanted be in the future and with whom. He said that he had been thinking a lot about us. He knew that I was a good woman and he didn't want to lose me. Then he asked what I would do if he were to ask me to marry him. At first, I was shocked and didn't really know what to say to him. Shawn had always been quite a ladies' man. Nevertheless, one thing I could say about him was that he never said or did anything that he didn't mean. No matter how many times I asked him questions about me being the only girl in his life, expecting him to lie, he never did.

Shawn would always say, "I told you who I was in the beginning, and you knew from the start that I didn't want to be in a serious relationship." Or, he would just call me by my name and that always meant, "Don't ask me that! I don't want to have to hurt your feelings with the truth." When the topic of marriage came up, I didn't know how to handle it. In response to my hesitation, he assured me that although he'd asked the question, he wasn't expecting an immediate answer. After we ended our call and in the days between our next call, I couldn't think of anything else but his question of marriage. It was evident from the tone of our conversation that he had thought a great deal about this.

Our next phone call started awkwardly with small talk about our daily activities and the children. Both of us seemed hesitant about bringing up marriage. Finally, he took control of the conversation and asked if I had thought about what he asked me during his last call. I readily admitted that it was all I'd thought about. I told him that if he was ready to commit, then so was I.

It took me about a week to tell my family. I wanted to wait until we'd completed all the required paperwork for inmates and prospective spouses, and was certain that everything was a go. I was never worried about them questioning or judging me. My family loved Shawn, but I knew that they would be just as shocked as I was that he really wanted to get married. When I broke the news to them, it was just as I had hoped. They were very happy for us and they were all very supportive. We had to wait a month for the prison to respond to our marriage petition. When we did receive a response, we learned that our wedding date was set for two months later. The prison assigned the wedding dates, and they only performed wedding ceremonies every four to five months. We were both happy, but still I couldn't believe that I was about to marry the man of my dreams in jail.

I had a lot to do before the big day. I had to get my hair done, find a dress to wear, and make sure that I had a babysitter for the weekend of our wedding. I had already spoken to my good friend Tejuana and talked her into taking the five-hour-long drive down to the prison with me. I found a nice, simple, cream dress and shoes to match.

Tejuana and I arrived at the prison about an hour before visiting hour began. This gave me time to rest and get dressed without rushing. When the time came for our ceremony, I was led into the room where Shawn was waiting for me. I felt the butterflies in my stomach as soon as I walked in the door and saw him standing there. The nervous smile on his face assured me that he was just a nervous as I was. The ceremony went by quickly, and the next thing I knew we were signing our marriage license.

We were only given a short period of time to spend with each other before he had to go back to his cell. We used those precious moments sitting together discussing everything we were going to do when he was released. Right before I left him, he looked me in my eyes and told me that if we ever broke up, it would be because I left him—because he was never going to leave me. That's when I knew for sure that I was in love with this man.

It was two months before I saw Shawn again. This visit would be different from the others and I was very excited. It would be our first conjugal visit. Spouses were allowed to stay for the entire weekend in a private house located across from the jail. In preparation for my weekend with Mr. Gamble, I went to the grocery store and bought everything he liked. I rented lots of DVDs and went over the list of rules about twenty times that the prison had sent me. It outlined all the things that were and were not allowed, and what I could and could not bring with me. I didn't mind all the harassment I would have to endure once I got there because we were about to be together for the first time as husband and wife.

It turned out to be a great weekend. I cooked for him, we watched every movie I'd brought and snuggled up under each other for the whole two days. When it was time for me to leave, it felt bittersweet. Even though I was ready to get back to my children, work, and my life on the outside, I didn't want to leave him. Knowing I would be back next month, I just sucked it up, gave him a great big kiss, and drove down the long road that took me back to the freeway.

On the drive back, I reminisced about my romantic weekend and being married to the man I loved. I smiled at every thought that came to mind about us—how we were just being silly and running around the house. When he caught me, I was laughing so hard as he threw me on the bed that I almost peed my pants. Hovering over me as I laid on the bed, Shawn looked into my eyes and gave me that loving look. Suddenly the silly mood changed, he grabbed me by my waist and kissed me very passionately. Those thoughts were almost as amazing as the experience.

I was so happy as I walked into my apartment. As soon as I put my bags down, I called the children at my sister Angie's house to check on them and told them I would be there to get them in a couple of days. I then took a long hot shower, lay down on my bed, and passed out. I fell asleep around two-thirty p.m. and didn't wake up until the next morning.

The next day went pretty smoothly. I got up and went running, then stopped by a local cafe and grabbed some breakfast. Afterwards, I came back home to lie down until I had to go to work. For some reason, I kept going in and out of sleep, unable to fall into a deep sleep. As I tried to sleep, Shawn called to make sure I had made it home safely. We talked a bit about our weekend, cracked a few jokes, and finally said our goodbyes.

As the months went by, I did anything I could think of to keep busy. In preparation for Shawn's release and my regaining custody of my children, I moved into a two bedroom. It was two stories, two bedrooms, one-and-a-half baths, with a huge living room and dining room. My friend Katrina was been living in the unit next door, so I knew the owner of the building. When I found out that I'd gotten the place, I worked nonstop for three months straight. I wanted to buy all new furniture throughout the house, decorate, and furnish the kid's room before they came home.

I was really happy with where my life was headed even though I was missing Shawn something fierce. No matter how much I worked, I still visited him as much as I could. We talked on the phone as much as possible. Unfortunately, it soon became apparent that something had to change. My phone bills were getting out of control, so we decided that we would only talk to each other twice a week instead of every day. I knew this would be hard for the both of us!

Chapter Four:
A Different Me!

One Thursday afternoon, I had to run to the Social Security office to take care of some paper work for Jamie. When I was done, I took the information that was needed and walked out toward my car. As I was about to get into my vehicle, someone said, "Excuse me, but do I know you?" I turned around slowly and took a good look at this person before answering. She didn't look familiar to me at all. So I said, "No!" She smiled and replied, "Oh! I'm sorry. I saw you looking back at me when you were leaving, so I thought I would come over and ask you if we knew each other." At first, I was about to let her know that it wasn't her I was looking at, but the paperwork the clerk behind the counter told me to pick up before I left. Instead, I smiled and got into my car. She then walked closer and said, "You know, I have never done this before, but do you think I could get your number?" I sat and thought about it for a second and was about to decline, but then I thought, *What the heck?* Then, for a split second, I thought, *This is a female who looks like a boy; give her the wrong number.* For some reason I decided against it and gave her my real number instead. She told me her name was Casey and that she would give me a ring soon.

The first few times my phone rang and Casey's number came up on the display, I felt a bit weird so I would let the calls go to voicemail. This went on for about two weeks before I eventually answered her call. I didn't really know what I was doing, but something inside of me wanted to see what she wanted and why she was being so persistent.

Casey and I talked on the phone every day for a few weeks before I let her come over. I really didn't want to be bothered, but at least she provided a distraction from thinking of Shawn every second of the day and feeling incredibly lonely. I allowed her to come over to my apartment so we could properly meet for the first time. At first, I didn't know what to expect. When she came to the door, she knocked once, then walked in without waiting for me to invite her in. I was going to say something smart to her; I didn't appreciate her just walking in without being invited. But I didn't say anything; I just looked at her and laughed. She introduced the young girl she'd brought with her as her little sister Cortina. Then she proceeded to show her sister around my house. I didn't really know how to take her boldness, but I was very intrigued by how she took charge. She left soon after she dropped by, but later called me and invited me to a movie playing later that evening.

After that night, Casey and I became inseparable. She made it her business to call me every morning and every night. She would meet me at my apartment after I took the children to school. She'd cook breakfast for me, then I would go back to sleep. When I went to sleep, she would leave and come back later when I was awake to clean up my house and cook dinner before I got ready to head back to work. As time passed, I started to get these weird feelings for her. I couldn't explain these feelings. I believed that I could keep them under control. I mean, for goodness sake! This was a girl, just like me, and there was no way I was going to allow myself to have feelings for a girl! Her family loved me and I was growing very fond of them as well. Casey's mom and sister would even watch the children for me while I worked—for free!

I tried very hard to keep my feelings in check, but they were growing stronger the more time we spent together. It got to the point where I couldn't deny it anymore. I was starting to fall for her in a way that wasn't right. I had never had anyone in my life this kind, helpful, understanding, and who treated me like a princess. There wasn't anything that this girl wouldn't do for me, my children, or my family. It got to the point where she would come over early to get the children dressed for school and drop them off so I wouldn't have to get out of bed. Afterwards, she would come back, clean my whole house as usual, then she'd run my bath. All I really had to do when she was there was come downstairs, eat, then get in the bath she'd prepared for me.

Casey eventually started staying at my house to watch the children while I was at work. She was so into me that she would call me at work to ask me what time I would be getting home. As soon as I walked into the house, I would find that my clothes were laid out in the bathroom and my bath water was ready. Then she would bring my dinner to me in bed and wait until I finished eating to take the dishes back down to the kitchen before she let herself out to go home. This routine would start all over again early the next morning. Things were getting pretty serious with us. I would look at her thinking I could be with her forever. I had no clue what I was going to do or why I was having these feeling. Casey knew I was married but she never let it bother her. That was until I had to sit her down and tell her that we were going to have to stop spending so much time together. Shawn was due to be released in another month. It was obvious that she was in love with me and I had strong feelings for her, too. Of course, she did not take the news well. She just sat on the couch in a daze for the rest of the day.

Those last few days seemed to fly by. Finally, the day came when I had to pick Shawn up from prison. It had seemed like the day would never come. It was a day of mixed emotion, happy that Shawn was coming home, but sad that my relationship with Casey was going to change. During the five-hour drive to pick up Shawn, I couldn't stop thinking about her. How in the world was I going to explain my friendship with her to Shawn? Would he be angry or would he understand? I decided not to bring it up until I felt it was an appropriate time to discuss it.

Still thinking about Casey and what I would say to Shawn, I tried rationalizing my relationship with this woman. I tried convincing myself that I was only hanging out with her to pass the time until Shawn came home. I knew for certain that I wasn't going to leave my husband for her, so this thing between me and Casey really didn't matter.

When I arrived at the jail, it took another two hours before I could see him. I had to wait for him to be processed and for all the paperwork to be done before we could actually go home. I was sitting in the waiting room when I saw him coming down the hall. I was so elated that I ran out the door leading to the hallway and jumped into his arms. On the drive home, Shawn and I held hands, enjoying the mountains and trees we passed along the way. When we arrived home, the children were there and he jumped out of the car to greet them as they ran toward him. I sat on the steps inside the house and daydreamed about how happy we were all going to be as a family.

As Shawn's family made their way over to welcome him home, he went upstairs to take a shower while I put all his things away. In doing so, I began to look through the photo albums he'd made for us while he was inside. Every time I flipped a page over, my smile got bigger and brighter. He had all these pictures of me and the children, and the letters I'd sent him over the years. There was only one more photo album left. Right before I put it down, I looked at the last page, and there was a picture of his ex-girlfriend—his first love. I pulled it out, took a closer look, then read the back of it. She had written, "Close your mouth. I know I look nice, but you will see this body again when you get home. Love, Your Girl." I sat there staring down at the picture for a minute. I simply didn't know what to say.

I waited for Shawn to come downstairs, held up the photo to his face, and asked him, "What is this?" He tried to say it wasn't anything, and to explain that her mother used to write him and decided to send him a picture. Upset and feeling betrayed, I threw the picture in his face and told him to tear it up. He didn't. Instead, Shawn told me, "If you want to throw it away, go right ahead, but I'm not going to do it!" He added that I was being silly and insecure about nothing. In that instant, something inside of me clicked off, and I felt my love for him run down the drain like pouring out sour milk.

For the next couple of weeks, Shawn looked for a job. The one thing I could definitely say about him was that he was a hard worker. He would always keep the house clean, cook for the children while I was at work, and fix anything that was broken. We got along pretty well and seemed to be getting closer, but I never really trusted him after finding the picture. I always felt that he was doing something behind my back, so I decided to continue my friendship with Casey. Shawn was never fond of my friendship with her. He would always tell me that he didn't want me hanging out with her. Even though I tried to stop, I couldn't let her go. I think it was largely due to the fact that whenever he made me feel he was up to no good, I would always talk to her about it and she would make me feel better.

One day, we were having family day. Shawn was helping the children get ready for bed and I was sitting in the bedroom while the children were running around the house. The phone rang and something told me to grab it but I didn't. Keithshon picked it up and told me it was

Casey. Caught off guard, I was just going to hang it up, but I couldn't find it in my heart to do it. When I got on the phone, she was being her normal self, cracking jokes and trying to make me laugh. After a few minutes, she realized that I wasn't saying much. I tried to make light of who was on the phone, so I got up and walked out of the room. Shawn knew it was her and looked at me, reminding me that he didn't want me talking to her anymore and to let her know that she wasn't allowed to call our home again. Without thinking about it twice, I repeated what he'd told me previously and hung up the phone. I didn't really know what else to do. After all, Shawn was my husband and he came first. I would not allow anyone to come between us.

Christmastime came and I was working overtime at the club. I was working so much that I really didn't have time to do much shopping or take the children to pick out a Christmas tree. Picking out a Christmas tree was a tradition we religiously observed every year together as a family. One evening, Shawn showed up at my job to pick me up early and told me to get my things so he could take me home. Surprised, I said, "No! It's really good tonight, plus I still have to get back on stage one more time." Determined to get his way, he stood firm and told me to get my things and come home right away. I told my boss that I was leaving early. I had no idea what was wrong, but I didn't feel like fighting with Shawn.

The children were in the car when I came out and they we really excited for some reason, but at the time I didn't pay it any mind. We drove off and before we got to the corner where we lived, everybody told me to close my eyes, so I did. Shawn parked the car, and the children grabbed my hand and helped me out of the car. I still had no idea what was going on. Once Shawn took his hand away from my eyes, I noticed I was standing in front of the big window of our home. All I could do was smile. They had gone and picked up a Christmas tree, put all the decorations on it, and had decorated the outside of the apartment. In that moment, it seemed like things between us were getting better. I started to believe that the love I once had for him could come back.

After that day when I would come home from work, Shawn would have candles lit and rose petals scattered on the stairs, in the bedroom, and in our bathroom. He made me feel like I was the best thing in the world. I was happy with Shawn, but I couldn't get past all the female friends he had and how he still kept secrets from me. I also felt that when it came to his son's mother, he did too much for her. Of course he would say it was for little Shawn, but I knew my husband. Sometimes he just didn't know how to say no, even if what he was doing for others would cause strife between us.

I recall an instance when Tejuana and I went out for her birthday, and we were dropped off at a club on Wilshire called the Shark Club. Shawn dropped us off in my car because he said he needed to take care of something then head home. After being at the club for a while, a fight broke out and we decided it would be better to leave. I called Shawn to tell him to come and get us, but I didn't get an answer. I called him back to back for about a half hour! Finally, I called his brother and told him to come get us because I couldn't find Shawn. His brother dropped me off at home. Shawn came in an hour later. I didn't say anything at first because I wanted to see what excuse he would have this time. After waiting for an hour, I finally asked him, "Where were you and why didn't you pick up your phone?" True to form, he gave me a lame excuse. "I was at my homeboy's house and left my phone in the car." Disgusted, I accepted the lie, knowing full well that one day the truth would come out. It didn't take very long for that to `happen.

I decided to take a day off work. I had been working non-stop for the past two weeks and just needed to relax. While I was outside cleaning out my car, I found an earring that didn't belong to me—in my car! I confronted Shawn and asked to whom it belonged. He finally told me that the day I was at the club, he couldn't come get me because he had taken his son's mother home. She would have had to catch the bus at eleven o'clock at night with the baby. He said that just wouldn't have been right. He was afraid we would argue over his decision. He knew I would get mad, so he chose to say nothing at all. He said he was very sorry that he'd kept it from me. After that club night, things between us started to change. Once again, no matter how hard I tried, I couldn't look at him the same. He was a good husband most of the time, but there were some things I couldn't let go of or deal with. I started hanging out with Casey again to keep my mind off the things that Shawn might have been doing. Every time he would do something else to hurt me or lie about something, it would push me even closer to her.

⟨∽∽⟩

Things between Shawn and I were going from bad to worse; no matter how hard we tried, it wasn't working out. One evening, I had just gotten home from work. We had been arguing earlier that day, and I was not looking forward to coming home. When I got there, he wasn't home. He had been out with his friends and didn't come in until late. We immediately started arguing. Instead of going downstairs to cool off, he said he wasn't coming back and left. I didn't even care.

After a few days passed, I thought that maybe we needed to talk to try to work it out. Whenever I called, he never picked up. I left voicemails, but he still didn't return my calls. After doing this for a week, I called his mother and told her what was going on, hoping that she would talk some sense into him by telling him to come home or call. Not so. She called me back twenty minutes later and said he was fine. My first thought was, *When is he coming home?* She never really said anything to shed light on the subject.

I called him one last time and he picked up. While talking to him, I realized that he was at the house of a so-called female friend whose mother liked him. I remember one night when he was hanging out over there and had called me from that number. Not knowing whose number it was at the time, I decided to store the number in my phone, just as I did every time he called from a number I didn't recognize. All of a sudden, the phone went dead. I called back and the girl's mother answered. When I asked if I could please speak to him, she dropped the phone and told Shawn, "Come and get the phone before I curse this b***** out for calling my house." Now, at that very moment, I was beyond pissed and told him that I was on my way to come pick him up. I also told him that I wasn't playing this game anymore and he'd better have his stuff ready. If I saw this woman when I got there, I was going to have a few words with her. I think he knew I was serious. When I pulled up, I parked my car and got out ready to walk into their house, but he started throwing his things into the car before I could walk up to the door. He grabbed me by the arm and put me back into the car.

Things were quiet with us for about a month, but I just didn't look at him the same. Even though he was at home when he wasn't working, it didn't seem to matter anymore after that last big blow up. I realized that I didn't want to go through this with him anymore. I decided to tell Shawn that it would be better if he left and we spent some time apart for a while. Even though I would miss Shawn, I knew that I could never truly trust him the way I needed to in order to make our marriage work. We tried to make it work while we were separated, but I would see him out at the club doing the same old thing that he'd has always done.

My oldest sister Yolanda was turning forty and she'd decided to celebrate by having a girls' night out at a male exotic strip club called, "The Fire House," on Florence Avenue in Los Angeles. It was getting late, and I was tired and ready to leave. I kissed everyone goodbye. My sister Eva and I left the club and headed home. I was driving down Crenshaw and something on my left side caught my attention. I looked over, seeing four cars that looked familiar. Without saying a word to Eva, I made a U-turn and pulled up in the island where all these guys were hanging out and talking. When I stopped right in front of Shawn's car, his brother Tyron ran over to block the window so I couldn't see the girl sitting in the front seat. I told him to move but he wouldn't. When I looked in my rear view mirror, I saw Shawn walking away from his car. I thought that I could do one of two things. I could get out of the car and beat the crap out of him and the girl, or I could just let it go. I looked over at my sister. She already had her heels off and told me that we could do whatever I wanted to do about the situation. In that moment, I thought, *I'm done with fighting over him.* I pulled off and didn't look back.

After going through so much hurt, lies, and pain with men, I thought to myself, *Why don't I just pursue a relationship with Casey?* She gave me everything I wanted and needed. She cooked, cleaned, helped with the children, and was willing to do anything that my family asked of her. She never complained about what I did and didn't do. Every night when I came home from work she gave me a full body massage and folded the covers down on my bed for me. When I got out of the bath, all I had to do was climb in my bed after a long day of work and fall asleep. After thinking about how good Casey was for me, I said to myself, "What the heck?" I deserve to be with someone who will treat me like the woman I am and love me the way I deserved to be loved. I had had it with men and as far as I was concerned, they were all the same: no good, cheating liars, and I wouldn't have anything else to do with them ever again!

Casey was so very happy when I told her that I wanted to give our relationship a try. She packed up all her things at her mom's house and moved in with me so we could be together every day. I had to admit I was very happy with her. I never thought I could be with anyone without having to deal with a bunch of drama. For the next couple of years we lived pretty well.

The club I was working at closed down for remodeling, and I didn't know how I was going to pay my bills. Luckily, the owner also owned two other clubs—The Blue Room, which was one of the top black clubs in Gardena, and King Jeffery's, which was just a few blocks away from The Blue Room. The girls from the club I worked at were going to work at one of the two during the remodel. King Jeffery's was where Big Bob, the manager, would send the girls who didn't fit his image of class. The Blue Room was very upscale, and he made sure that he handpicked the ladies to represent him and the club. I heard that he had made a list of girls chosen to work at The Blue Room. I never even bothered to check to see if my name was on it. I never thought that I was pretty enough to work at The Blue Room. I automatically assumed I'd end up at King Jeffery's.

A week after the club closed, I got a phone call from Cali, one of the girls from the old club, asking when I was scheduled to start working at The Blue Room. I told her that I had no clue and that I was looking for a new club to work at. Surprised by my response, she asked, "Why? Didn't you know you were one of the first girls the manager picked"? That meant a lot coming from him, since he was known for his very particular taste. I was only dancing at The Blue Room for a few weeks before I was making more money than I could count. I already had a brand new Expedition that I'd paid cash for right off the lot before I'd left the old club. With all that new money, I was able to by new rims and have an expensive stereo system installed. I was living pretty well, and there wasn't anything I couldn't buy for my children or myself. Every birthday or holiday, I would buy myself the hottest new limited-edition boots at Charles David, or the new signature Tiffany necklace. My children had any and everything that they wanted. I promised myself after the fire that my children would never suffer again or want for anything.

During this high time of my life, I decided that I wanted to go back to school to become a nurse. I knew I wasn't going to be able to dance forever, so I thought nursing was a good career to pursue. The decision to go back to school couldn't have come at a better time. I made my own schedule, Casey helped with the children, and I was in a good financial position.

A couple of months before I was supposed to graduate from nursing school my Aunt Bert became sick. No one really knew how bad it was until she had to stop working. That's when she knew she had to tell us that she had ovarian cancer. I made it a point to sit with her to make sure she ate regularly, and helped her to get dressed whenever she needed me to. I drove her wherever she needed to go, and if I couldn't do it, then Casey would do it for me.

Aunt Bert became progressively worse and had to be admitted into the hospital. While in the hospital, she was quite stubborn and wouldn't let anyone take care of her. She would let everyone know that her niece was a nurse. I would go to the hospital to bathe her and take care of her. She was always so happy when she saw me walking in for a visit, even though she was only there for three days. Once they released her, I made sure that everything was ready for her arrival at her home.

My sisters and I all took turns helping Aunt Bert. Whether it was taking care of her paperwork, cooking, combing her hair, or just making sure she was comfortable. We were all working together. I was so happy she wanted me to help her get better. My aunt was never the kind of person who would let anyone do anything for her. She was known as the one in the family who took care of everything and everyone else. Honorable and extremely stubborn, that was my Aunt Bert. We didn't even find out she was as sick as she was until it was too late; we all thought she was going to recover.

The following Wednesday, as I was leaving school, something told me to call my aunt to see if she wanted me to bring her something to eat. I went home first, figuring I could do some homework, then go check on her later. Fifteen minutes later, my phone rang and Casey told me it was my sister Eva. When I picked up the phone, I heard Eva crying. She was very upset and I could barely make out what she was saying. I told her to calm down so I could understand her. I was finally able to make out her pleas for me to come to her house quickly. She kept saying, "I really need you to come now!"

Concerned, I told Casey I would be right back and drove around the corner. As I pulled up to my aunt's house, Eva was standing outside. When I walked up to her, she explained that my uncle had told her that my aunt was on her way to the bathroom but she never made it. She collapsed by the front door and never got up. When Eva went to check on her she realized that she wasn't breathing. She tried to finish telling me the rest of the story, but she couldn't finish. She was grabbing her stomach, gasping for air. Eva was crying too hard to talk to me. After a few seconds, she told me that I needed to call everyone and let them know about what had happened. She kept repeating, "I can't do this. I need you to take care of this."

I walked into the house, dreading what I would find. As soon as I stepped in the door, I saw my aunt lying on the floor not moving. I walked over to her, checked for a pulse and, of course, there wasn't one. All I could do at that point was say a prayer. I grabbed my cell phone and called Angie, Yolanda, Andrea, and Christina. I told them that they needed to get over to Aunt Bert's house right away. Once everyone arrived, we sat around and just looked at our aunt. The woman who had given up everything to raise us was lying on the floor, lifeless. I wanted to cry but I couldn't. I knew that my day would come when the tears would flow freely and unchecked. Not that day! I needed to be strong for whoever needed me.

It took about three hours before the coroner came to pick up her body. Before they took my aunt away, I asked them to give us a moment. I told everyone to stand in a circle around her, grab hands, and close their eyes so we could pray over her before we allowed her to go on to her reward.

My oldest sister Yolanda took care of the funeral arrangements. She was always good at things like that. She had done it for our mother who died from complication with AIDS back in 2002. We knew she would plan a beautiful homegoing for our beloved Aunt Bert.

Chapter Five:
The Transition

Throughout the years with Casey, I was repeatedly unfaithful. I dated a doctor who was much older than me. I knew it wasn't right to cheat on Casey, but deep down I missed being in the company of a man. Despite it all, Casey treated me very well.

Admittedly, I had abandonment issues. I was very broken and insecure. When I met the doctor at The Blue Room, I thought he was a good guy. We would laugh and talk for hours. After I would get off the stage from dancing, we would go into the private room and just hang. Most of the time, he didn't even want a dance. He would just pay me to sit and talk. When we started seeing each other outside of the club, I looked at him as healing for my soul. I didn't want to be with him, but there was something about him that made me feel that, one day, I could find a man of my own to make me feel the way he made me feel. Until that time came, I told myself I would have fun. I had Casey pampering me when I was home, and the doctor pampering me when I was away from home. Dating the doctor came with many perks. I was going to basketball games during playoff season, sitting in the front row. I even took some of my family members with me to New York for the weekend to see a play on Broadway. We stayed at a five-star hotel, and everything was paid for, compliments of the doctor.

When I wasn't traveling, I was doing music videos, modeling, and car shows. I had parts in movies and I was featured in the hottest magazines. I thought nothing could stop me. I loved knowing that whenever I spent too much money, I was able to go to work, dance at the club, and make it up. But I hated the drama that came with working with nothing but females. There was always something going on at work. Girls were always arguing in the dressing room over a customer. Sometime fights broke out because one of the girls danced with another girl's customer. There was an unspoken rule that if a guy came in to see and dance with a certain girl all the time, he was off limits to everyone else. We knew to respect the code of making money, but when it was slow or really busy, that rule would go out the door if the guy kept following you around asking for a dance. These actions resulted in girls' cars being keyed, tires slashed, and girls being beaten up in the parking lot of the club or even stabbed in the eyes with stiletto heels. The club life was starting to wear on me heavy; I started going to work less and less. I also stopped dating the doctor after his wife found out about us. Working fewer hours and not dating hit my pocket hard. Although I was bringing home much less money, I didn't care. I needed a change from all this chaos. I felt lost and confused.

The next morning I called Casey's cousin, Lizzy, and told her I would take her up on her repeated offers over the last few months to attend church with her. The Monday before I was set to attend church with Lizzy, I was at home cuddled up on the couch with my dog, Foxy. The children were in bed and Casey was working late. I found a good old movie on TV. As I sat there alone watching it, I couldn't help getting lost in the love scenes. As I watched the man and woman in the movie making love, I found myself wishing that was my life. Sadly, I thought, *What have I done? What I have with Casey is not what I want for my life. I miss the smell of a man and having his big strong arms around me while hugging and squeezing me. I want to be able to have more children.* That's when I said it aloud, "This isn't right!"

I left work early that Saturday night because I wanted to get some sleep and get up early for church the next morning. I had been feeling really down all that week and I knew church was just what I needed.

I loved El Shaddai Christian Church. I had been attending for about a year. Whenever I was going through something, I knew that once I got to church, the Word for that day would be just for me. When I walked out of those church doors, I would be a brand new person. Even though I wasn't raised in church, there was something about being in the presence of God that made me feel as if everything was going to be all right.

I remember being at church one Sunday morning, eyes closed and worshipping, when this voice kept popping up in my head, saying, "Give fifty dollars to the pastor." At first, I just thought I was tripping, until I heard it over and over again. This time the voice said, "If you trust Me, watch what I will do for you if you give." Of course, I thought I was going nuts talking to myself and then answering myself. Then I thought, *What's the worst that can happen?* So I gave.

I usually took Sunday night off at the club, but after giving up my last fifty dollars, I decided to go in to work and make some extra money for the week. When I walked in the club, it was slow. There were only nine girls working; normally, there would be at least fifteen to twenty girls working. As I looked around the club, I only saw twelve customers. Despite it being a slow night, I decided to stay.

I did two shows and had some free time to sit with one of the regular customers to have a drink. After my last show, I sat in the corner and counted the money I'd collected. To my surprise, I'd made fifteen hundred dollars. I had only been at the club for two hours! As I sat there amazed, I was reminded of the words I'd heard at church earlier, "If you trust Me, watch what I will do for you." I couldn't believe it. I went home early that night. I worked every day that week and made more money that week than the whole month all together. When Saturday came, I decided to take the night off and chill. I wanted to be well rested for church on Sunday.

After I left church, I was hungry and called my friend Kyle to see if he wanted to get some lunch with me. I really didn't want to go home and see Casey, so I dropped the children off and headed to the Cheesecake Factory in Marina Del Rey. I was always very happy to see Kyle. He and I had been hanging out for about seven months. We could always make each other feel better about things going on in our lives. He was the second guy who I'd met in the club who I enjoyed hanging out with. There were so many men who had tried to pay for my attention, but only two had succeeded in the eleven years I'd been dancing.

I was having serious doubts about my lifestyle and my relationship with Casey; he was having issues at home as well. Kyle was preparing to leave his wife. Knowing we could call on one another for moral support, we promised to be there no matter what. I thought Kyle was a great guy. He listened to me, he was smart, and I loved the way he dressed. He had his own style that served him well and made him look like he'd stepped out of a GQ magazine. He had curly black hair, which was neatly kept, and the cutest glasses. I noticed that whenever he took his glasses off he couldn't see a thing; I thought that was the cutest thing ever. I also liked the fact that he was a fifth-grade teacher.

He was different from the guys I normally dated. He opened me up to new things, different genres of music, interesting books, fashion and exotic foods. He introduced me to the music of Dwele and Raheem DeVaughn. I began to read books by T.D. Jakes and Joel Olsteen. Kyle would surprise me with the hottest shoes and sandals that he wanted to see me in. He would say that all he could do was imagine me wearing them out on one of our dates. I was starting to believe that maybe, just maybe, there were still some good guys out there after all.

One day Kyle's wife sent me an email. She told me that I was going to get what I deserved for messing with a married man, and that everything that he was telling me was a lie. I was so caught up in him and what he'd told me that I deleted her message and told him to deal with her. I had nothing to do with their relationship. Besides, he and I were just friends. Anyway, I wasn't trying to marry him! For the life of me, I never thought he would lie to me; he had no reason to. He told me that the only reason he was still with his wife was because of the children. Since I was going through something similar with Casey, who was I to judge him? At that point my relationship with Kyle wasn't sexual. Truth be told, it was more of an emotional affair than anything. Neither one of us was ready to leave our relationships, so we decided to keep seeing each other, platonically.

Kyle and I spent every moment we could together when he wasn't working. We talked on the phone every day while he was at work, and he would come to the club to see me almost every night when I worked. Sometimes, we would get a hotel room to spend time alone, to watch a movie or play video games. Other times we would take a trip out of town for a couple of days.

I felt as if I was caught between two worlds. I knew I needed to find a way to leave the one I was in with Casey, but the one I was falling into was just as wrong. Needing so badly to escape from Casey, I didn't care how my relationship with Kyle was affecting his wife or children. I was selfish and wanted to do what made me happy. I longed to break free from this world I'd built for myself. Whatever I was going through, Kyle was right there with me, holding my hand, telling me that everything would be o.k. He assured me that I was doing the right thing by leaving my relationship with Casey.

Casey always knew that I had a special friendship with Kyle, but she would never ask for any details. I never had to tell her anything. I knew that I couldn't stay with Casey any longer. I had fallen out of love with her about a year prior, and it had been at least eight months since we'd slept in the same bed. She would come home from work, sit on the couch, smoke her weed, and watch television as I was heading out of the house to go hang out with whomever. It got to the point that I would come home just to cook dinner, spend time with the children, and get ready for work. On my days off, I stayed in the bedroom while she fell asleep on the couch, not even bothering to wake her to come to bed. This routine became our way of life. Soon, reality hit me hard, and I knew I had to do something fast. I didn't want to hurt her, but I had also decided that this type of relationship wasn't right for me anymore.

I got down on both knees one Saturday night and said a desperate prayer to the Lord. I really didn't know how to pray, so I just asked Him to help me because I couldn't go on like this much longer.

Church seemed to be going quite strong when I got there Sunday morning. Praise and worship was going forth, and even though it was a small church, it was full this Sunday. I found a seat on the second row with Lizzy. As the Spirit moved me, I stood there with my eyes closed and talked to God. My heart was so heavy that I couldn't pay proper attention.

There was a guest speaker there that morning. She asked for all the young people to come up so they could receive prayer. Well, since I didn't consider myself to be all that "young" anymore, I stayed seated. A few seconds later, I felt a pat on my back and it was Pastor White asking me if I had gone up for prayer. Responding "No" with a hesitant smile, he nudged me and told me to go on up there.

I walked up there with no expectations, just doing what I had been asked by my pastor.

While I stood there waiting my turn for prayer, all I could think about was getting back to my seat. I never liked going up in front of the church; I felt like people were always watching me with judgment in their hearts. Right before I could finish my thought, this woman was standing in front of me staring into my eyes. Initially, Pastor Shaw didn't say anything, but when she finally opened her mouth and spoke, I was truly astonished. She declared, "I don't know you or what you are going through, but there is a major decision that you need to make and God is telling me to tell you that you need to make it today, or there will be major consequences that you are going to deal with."

At that moment, tears rolled down my face and I felt my knees give way under me as I fell to the floor. After that, all I remember was weeping and screaming as I cried out to God. I begged Him to help me break free, to take away the pain and guilt that I was feeling. I told Him I didn't want to live this life anymore, but I needed Him to direct my footsteps and take me where He needed me to go. My heart was so heavy that I couldn't even lift my head off the floor. Giving it all to Him, I asked for the strength to do what I needed to do to walk away from my nine-year lesbian relationship with Casey.

Feeling as if I wasn't in my body any longer, I lay on the floor unable to move. I was still quite aware of all these feet around me standing in a circle praying for me. This went on for about 45 minutes, maybe even the rest of the service. Laid out on the floor unable to move, I had never experienced anything this intense in my life. Much later, when I was able to get up, I felt light as a feather.

Equipped with a new outlook, it seemed as if everything I had gone through for the past few months was gone. It was time for me to start a new life. The drive home that day was the longest I had ever taken. I understood what had to be done, yet I was really afraid to do it. There was no way around it but to tell her the truth. I knew this would crush Casey. She had always told me that I was everything to her. Memories of those heartfelt words made me even sorrier that I was going to hurt her so badly—the very thing I had tried to avoid doing for so long. She had been so good to me and my children. Frankly, I didn't love her anymore. There were so many things I wanted and needed to do with my life that I knew I could never do with her.

Then there was Casey's family to consider. They had been my other family for the past nine years also. Her mom had been there for me the first Mother's Day after my own mom passed away in 2002. Even though this was tough, I still had to go through with it. When I walked through the door, she was sitting on the couch watching television. She got up, came over to me, gave me a kiss, and asked how church service had gone, just as she did every Sunday. This time my reaction was different; I didn't answer her question. I just walked straight to the bedroom, closed the door, and sat on the edge of my bed for three hours until I could get the nerve to have "the talk."

Kyle had been calling my cell phone constantly that day, but I couldn't talk to him either. I was too drained from what had happened at church and what was about to take place at home. Even though I really wanted to hear his voice and let him tell me that everything was going to be okay, I knew that he was just going to have to wait.

It was about four p.m. when I finally came out of the bedroom and told Casey that we needed to talk. Concerned, she followed me back into the bedroom, sat down next to me on the bed, and asked what was wrong. I tried to speak but nothing came out at first. Taking a deep breath, I began speaking slowly and told her that I loved her but I couldn't do this anymore and that it was time for us to go our separate ways. I explained how I thought it would be best if she went to stay with her mom for a while. I didn't even look at her when I said it because I already knew how she would take it. As I left the bedroom, I looked over my shoulder before closing the door and noticed she was just sitting in the corner, allowing the tears to flow down her face. My first instinct was to run back to her, wrap my arms around her, and console her. Deciding it would only make the situation much worse, I grabbed my keys and went for a drive until it was time to pick up the children from her mom's house.

Needing alone time, I took off work for a few days. I wasn't ready to face people yet. All I wanted to do was sit on my couch and cry myself to sleep. Casey had moved out the day after our discussion. Kyle called me every day to check on me and even came by a couple of times after work to spend some time with me. I felt lost and relieved at the same time.

Casey and I talked a few times after her departure. She promised that she would help me out by watching the children until I could find a permanent babysitter. Despite her promise, when I was ready to go back to work, she was nowhere to be found. When I did manage to contact her, she informed me that she had changed her mind, deciding it would be best for her peace of mind not to do anything else to help me. She thought that I really needed to figure it out on my own and leave her out of the equation. I was disappointed but I understood that she also needed to cut all ties with me to get over our relationship. I hung up the phone, went outside, and sat on the stoop, looking up at the stars and talking to God. I told him that I needed His help, and I didn't know how I was going to be able to work without someone to take care of my children. If I couldn't work, how would I be able to pay my bills?

For the past nine years, I had depended on Casey to do everything for me. How could I possibly do all of this without her? I was desperately seeking answers, so I sat looking up at the sky. The next couple of days I called everyone I could think of to help me with the children, but no one could. Just when I was ready to give up, my niece Tiffany volunteered to look after them until I could make more permanent arrangements. She said she could watch them for a few days. Now, she wasn't the most reliable person in the world, but I figured since I had done so much for her, this was a good time for her to return the favor. I was more than willing to pay her. Originally, she said she would be more than happy to do this for me. Yet, true to form, she didn't show up or even call to let me know that she couldn't make it. When I called her, every call went straight to voicemail.

Finally, I knew there was only one thing I could do. I had a talk with Eva. A few days before, she'd told me that I needed to let the children stay home by themselves, in her opinion they were old enough: Keithshon was thirteen and Jamie was ten. She claimed that I sheltered them too much, and the only way they would learn some responsibility was for me to let them stay home alone. I was extremely nervous at work all that night. I tried my hardest to keep myself busy by doing as many lap dances as I could and socializing as much as possible, just so I wouldn't be worried about the children. I called them every fifteen minutes to make sure they were okay.

Finally, I was able to work without worrying when they fell asleep. I had not left my children alone since the fire, so this was one on the hardest things I had done in a really long time. As time went by, things got easier. I didn't work as much, but when I did, I went in focused and made as much money as I could. I saved every penny I made. I wanted to move into a better place. I was having problems with the new owner of the house where we currently lived.

Kyle had finally left his wife and moved in with his best friend Luther. It was time for a change for us both. It took a while for me to find a new house, but it wouldn't be ready for about three months. During this waiting period, Kyle went with me when I bought all new furniture for the new place.

On Father's Day weekend, I had just gotten home from church and Kyle was waiting for me at my house. He had sold his black Chevy truck and wanted me to take him to the dealer to pick up his new car. He ended up purchasing another Chevy truck, just smaller. He wanted to downgrade to save money. I changed my clothes and dropped him off. After leaving him, I headed straight home since I had so much to do that day. I was moving into the new place that day and I still had to finish packing. I went back and forth taking whatever would fit in my car. We were operating like a normal couple, running errands and taking on daily challenges together.

Kyle didn't get back to my house until late that night, but I was happy to see him. I couldn't really enjoy his new truck because I was too tired from all the moving. I only had a few more things to take over and asked him to help with the last few boxes. He agreed, but I noticed he wasn't saying much or acting like his normal self. I didn't think much about his silence at first. Not until we were on our way back to the house. I asked him a question and he snapped at me. He said, "You're not the only one who is tired! I've been out all day." I looked at him as if he was crazy at first, and was about to say something; instead, I kept my mouth shut.

The next morning, I waited for Kyle to come help me move the last of my things, but when I called his phone, he didn't pick up. I left him a message and waited for him to call me back. He didn't call back until later that night. The first thing I asked when I heard his voice was where had he been all day. I couldn't believe he gave me attitude. He said that he was with his children and their mother, and they had taken the girls to the movies. When I asked why didn't he call and tell me this before, his response was, "Now I can't hang out with my children?" I didn't even bother to dignify that response with an answer. Instead, I just hung up the phone and finished doing what I needed to do. I was not going to fight with him about this. I needed to get ready for work.

Despite my encounter with Kyle, I was certain it would be a great night. Whenever I was having a bad day, I would go to work, dress really pretty, and let all the guys fall over me like sick little puppies—and get paid for doing it. I can't explain it, but it always made me feel powerful knowing that men would do anything for a woman with a nice figure and a pretty face.

Kyle and I weren't hanging out when I moved into my new place. After the stunt he'd pulled—not picking up his phone and thinking it was o.k. to spend the entire day with his ex-wife and not tell me anything—I decided to take some time apart from him to get myself settled. When the new furniture came, it made me think of him because we'd picked it out together. Things didn't seem the same since I was in the new house without him. I had gotten accustomed to the back and forth with him. I knew things would start to change once I showed him I had feelings for him. He knew all my secrets, and would play on my emotions every chance he got. At one point, he'd asked me about moving in together; but no matter how damaged I was on the inside, I knew that I wasn't ready to shack up with anyone. When I told him that, he started showing his true colors. After that, I did what I always did when men broke my heart. I cried myself to sleep and moved on.

My life was about to take a major turn, and God was up to something. At the time, I had no clue what it was. One night at work, things were different. I just couldn't make any money. It was extremely slow and all I wanted to do was go home. I sat in the dressing room most of the time and slept. When it was my turn to go on stage, I acted like I didn't hear them calling me to perform.

While going down the stairs to see if any of my customers had come in, I heard a voice in my head tell me to go and tell my boss Big Bob that I was quitting in August after my birthday party. At first, I just ignored it and kept walking, but when I got back into the dressing room, I heard it again. This time, it was so loud that I thought someone was standing next to me talking. I asked aloud, "If I do that, what will I do for money?" Then the voice said, "I'm going to take care of you!" Amazed, I asked, "So what will I tell people when they ask me why am I quitting?" I heard the voice say, "Tell them that you're going to step out on faith. Go downstairs and tell your boss you're quitting, because once you speak it out loud, then you're going to have to go through with it."

I walked downstairs slowly and very confused. I went over to my boss and told him that after my party in August, I was going to give it all up and walk away. Initially, he tried to talk me out of it. He told me that I needed to take a break for a while, and I would be back once my money ran low. I told him that I was serious and it was time for me to leave. He didn't say anything, but he had this worried look in his eyes. I mean, I had already convinced about eight girls to come to church with me and a few of them had even became members. Most of the time, I was preaching to encourage the girls at work anyway. He wished me luck and told me that he was going to miss me. That meant a lot coming from him because he was never nice to anyone. He was known as the boss from hell.

What's your Fantasy's
06 B-Day Bash.

Date:
Sat. Aug. 19
Time:
7pm – 2am

Free Food

Dress code strictly inforced
No white Tee's

For the next five months, I was busy planning for my big going-away birthday party. I was really excited. In the eleven years I had been dancing, I had never taken a break. Even though a lot of the girls would take off for months at a time to rest and then come back ready to do it all over again, that was never my motto. If I was ever going to take a break, it would be for good. I was so happy to know that I would be able to sit at home on a Friday night, put my feet up, watch television, and fall asleep when I got tired. The only thing I did before my big going-away birthday bash was work and sleep. I needed to make as much money as I could, and it was important to save every dime that I could.

August came around fast and I was ready for my big day. I went out to eat with some of my girls and then headed back to the house for our big night out. My good friend Raven rented a limo for me and picked me up at my house with around fifteen of the girls that I was close with from the club. We headed to a popular club in Century City. Kyle and some of his friends came along, but it didn't matter because it was my night and it was all about me.

When Shawn showed up with his cousin, I was happy to see him. We had decided to stay friends over the years, and would talk every now and again. Actually, we never truly stopped loving each other, but I knew it would never work. When he saw me dancing, he made his way over to me and pulled me away so we could have a few drinks together, talk, and just chill. Of course, Kyle was getting jealous because he wasn't used to someone else getting all of my attention. He tried to stay by my side all night. It was getting late and I was ready to go home. I think I had a little bit too much to drink that night. We all headed toward the limo. Before I could get in, Shawn came over to me and told me that he wanted to come home with me and spend the night. Even though I was tempted, I declined, knowing that it wouldn't be a good idea to hook up with him.

Once we pulled up to my house, I tried to get out of the car, but I kept stumbling. Then, I saw Kyle come over to the limo. He picked me up to carry me into the house. He had followed us back to my house. Even though I didn't want to be bothered with him either, I knew that he was going to be very attentive since I hadn't paid him any mind all night. He wasn't going to stop chasing me until he got what he wanted. This was just another one of our games we played with each other. Kyle couldn't get over the fact that Shawn was all over me, and he didn't want him to have any chance at hanging out with me. He even went so far as to call off work that next morning. He ended up staying with me that whole week helping me get ready for my big finale at the Blue Room.

Although I was happy and ready to move on with my life, something was telling me that maybe I wasn't ready to leave the club yet. I mean, I had just moved into my new place two months before, my rent was eleven hundred a month, and even though I had been saving, what would I do once the money ran out? What kind of job would I be qualified to get? Yes, I had my nursing certificate, but I was only a CNA. I started thinking that I should work until Christmas and save up more money and then stop. Saturday came around very fast, and I was so ready to get this day over with. I didn't have much to do, so I chilled around the house until it was time to get ready for work. Everyone met at my house so we could go in together. Kyle insisted on driving, so that I could have fun and not worry about driving home if I decided to have a drink. When I got to the club, it was already packed. People that I hadn't seen in years had come out to say their goodbyes. I walked around, took pictures, then got ready for my first big performance.

After coming off the stage for the first time that night, I stayed upstairs for a minute to cool off. When I went back down, Kyle was sitting in the corner looking upset. I walked over to him and asked what was wrong. He told me that he didn't feel comfortable; he felt as if I didn't want him there because I hadn't paid him much attention. In the back of my mind, I knew exactly where this was coming from. I stood there with him for a few minutes, and we took a few pictures together. Afterwards, I told him that I had to walk around and thank my customers. I had two more sets on stage and I knew I had to make these last shows good.

After my last show I was very tired, so I collected all my money, tied it into a plastic bag and asked Kyle to hold it until I could say my farewells and collect all my belongings. It was a long night and I was glad it was over, but I was still thinking that I would just take a few days off, then quit in December. When I woke up the next morning, it was like that whole life in the club had disappeared out of my heart. I had no desire to step foot back in there. August 19, 2006, was the day I officially walked away from it all!

I didn't do much initially after leaving the club. My life consisted of my children and church. Strangely, once I decided to make some drastic changes in my life, bad things just kept happening. Jamie was starting to give me hell, and getting kicked out of every school she attended for getting into fights. She started ditching school, talking back, and trying to fight with me.

Keithshon was in a private school that Kyle had gotten him into because no other school would take him. He was on his way out of that school for fighting as well. At least I had one bright spot in my life: I was really happy when Kyle started coming to church with me; he told me he was ready to act right and start a new life with me and the children. But things were getting hard for me in every other aspect of my life.

My money was running very low. After I quit the club, I paid off all my bills, took care of some debts to clear up my credit, took both cars in to have major tune-ups, and brought new tires for the SUV. I didn't want to worry about anything for a while until I decided my next move. Slowly but surely, Kyle began to act weird again. I really didn't have the time or energy to try to figure him out, even though he was helping me out with the bills while I looked for another job. Fear set in, and I was starting to think that maybe I had made the wrong decision by leaving the club the way I had. I knew I had heard a word from God telling me that He was going to take care of me. For some reason, I started to doubt myself and Him.

Our annual women's church conference was coming up and I was very excited to attend, but I didn't have any money to take with me. My good friend Lashawn was renting a car, so I didn't have to drive. She knew I didn't really have money to put gas in my truck. Two nights before I left for the conference, I was sitting in the hallway inside my house. The children were with my sister, and I was home alone—sad, broke, and very lonely. I started to think about everything. I was leaving in two days and didn't have a dollar in my pocket, rent was due in a week, and I had no clue how I was going to pay it. Bills were coming in and all I could do was throw them in a stack. Both of my cars were on empty and there was barely enough food in the house for the rest of the week. At that moment, tears started falling down my face faster than the water at Niagara Falls.

I lay down on the floor right where I was sitting and screamed out to God. I yelled and told Him that this was His doing. He had made a promise to me that if I left the club and walked away from my relationship with Casey, He would take care of me. Look at me now! I just moved into this place and I can't pay my rent or bills. I was so mad! I couldn't believe I was going through this, and I didn't want to trust God or live any more for that matter. I had no clue where my life was going and what was going to happen to me. Right when I thought about giving up, the phone rang and it was Kyle. He said that he was on his way to come by to bring me some money so I would have something in my pocket during my trip just in case I needed anything.

I picked myself up off the floor and lay down on the couch until Kyle arrived. Once he got there, we talked for a few minutes, and he told me to enjoy myself and try not to worry about anything. Then he said something weird. He told me not to call him while I was gone. He said that he just wanted me to focus on the conference. Even though I wanted to ask him what he meant, I didn't. I was so drained from crying that I just said, "Whatever," and went to bed.

The day of the conference, I was very excited, especially since a girl who'd left the club right after me and joined the church was going, too. I knew she was special the first time I saw her in the dressing room at The Blue Room. After I asked her name, I told her, "There is something about you. I don't quite know what it is, but you don't belong in this place." That was all she wrote! We had been there for each other ever since.

It was very hot in Palm Springs, but I didn't care because I was ready to have fun and be blessed, all at the same time. I didn't know what to expect but I was ready for whatever. I figured things were so bad with me that the only other way had to be up. Once we checked into our rooms, we went downstairs to see if any of the elders needed help, and of course, they did. We helped set up for opening night. Before I could leave, our First Lady, Sister White, pulled me aside and asked me if I would do her a favor. The first thing she asked was if I would be the Mistress of Ceremonies for the second night, and would I mind singing the song that I sang at my Ministry and Leadership Training Class graduation. This was an eight-month class our Pastor taught on the meaning of being in leadership in the ministry; it helped us learn our role and duties in the church. It also explained why we must serve before we can lead and how God loves to use the broken vessels to minister his word.

I didn't want to initially, but after thinking about all that I was going through, I figured it might make me feel better. After getting dressed, I went downstairs just in time for Praise and Worship. I had never seen such power and praise in one room. We danced, laughed, and sang. When it was time for me to go up, Sister White asked me to give a little testimony about my life before I sang the song she'd requested. As I got up and started walking to the front, I was very nervous. Even though I was enjoying myself, I wasn't ready to stand in front of anyone and talk. I tried to put on a good face, but the truth was I was hurting badly on the inside. Yet, I had already told her I would do it and knew I had to suck it up and do the best I could.

I shared about how I was an exotic dancer for eleven years, and in a relationship with a girl for nine. But when I came to El Shaddai, the Lord told me that I was going to have to walk away from it all. So I went from making a nice amount of money each month to nothing. I also explained that my rent and bills were due, and I had no clue how I was going to pay for any of it. I testified that I was tired and weak, and just wanted to give up. Then I started to sing *I Just Can't Give Up Now* by Mary Mary. I didn't make it through the whole song because I started crying and had to stop singing.

After I took my seat, Lashawn grabbed my hand and held it. It was time for the first preacher to go up and start the conference. I really didn't pay her any mind because I had my head down in my hands trying to stop the tears. Then I heard someone say, "Young lady, come up here," but I wasn't paying attention. Then she said it again, so I looked up and realized that she was talking to me. I wiped my face and walked up to the front of the room. She told me that everything was going to be okay and that God was going to bless me for doing what He said to do. She then said, "I heard you say that you don't have your rent money?" I said, "No." Then she asked when it was due. I told her on the third of the month. What happened next would forever change the way I saw how powerful God really is. She asked, "How much is your rent?" Startled, I told her that it was eleven hundred dollars. That's when she started shouting and praising the Lord. I didn't understand why she was doing it until she stopped and said, "I told the Lord a few months ago that I wanted to start giving more in my tithes and offering This year I want to give over a thousand dollars, whether I have it or not, so I am going to write you a check and pay your rent." I just fell to the floor and thanked God.

Everyone in the room started shouting, praising, and worshipping the Lord. I was so overwhelmed that I couldn't even walk back to my seat. Once I did find the strength, it didn't stop there. Before I could lift my head up, a young lady across the room got up from her table and came over to me and put some money in my hand. Then, one by one, people started to get up all over the room, coming over to me, putting money in my hand. It was so much that someone had to give me a bag so I could hold it all. I was crying so hard for so long that my face was dry from the salty tears. When I finally caught my breath, another minister came up to the podium and began to speak. She called me up again and starting talking to me. She said that while she was sitting down watching everything that was going on, the Lord told her to let me know that I was going to have a powerful praise dance ministry. In addition, I was also going to minister to young women living in a homosexual lifestyle. They would hear my story and decide to come out of it and be set free. When I heard that, I passed out.

After the conference was over, I was exhausted. All I could do on the ride back home was sleep. When I made it home, I wanted to call Kyle and tell him everything. I still couldn't believe it. I figured if I kept talking about it then it would become more of a reality. I sent him a text when I was fifteen minutes from the house and told him he could head over there and meet me. We sat and talked for a couple of hours. After awhile, I told him that I really wanted to go to bed. I knew that I needed to be at church bright and early so I gave him a big hug goodnight and locked up.

When I got up the next morning, my face was extremely dry from the heat in Palm Springs and all the crying. I looked at myself in the mirror and thought, *How in the world was I going to church looking like this?* No matter what kind of moisturizer I put on, it just didn't seem to work. I was not going to let this stop me from going, so I pulled my hair back in a ponytail, threw on a blouse and jeans, and headed out the door. When I walked in, everyone was having a good time and I knew it was going to be a great service. Pastor really didn't preach that day because of all the worshipping and testimonies.

The next morning, I was doing some work on the computer when my phone rang. It was the lawyer who was helping Eva to sell our grandmother's home on 2nd Avenue. This matter had been going on for so long that I had forgotten all about it. I had to force myself to remember who this person was. Once I did, she told me to come down to her office because she was ready to distribute the proceeds from the sale. We all were under the impression that we were only getting around three thousand dollars each. But when I got down to the office and looked at my check, it was made out for sixty-five hundred dollars. I broke down right there in the lawyer's office. Surprised, she gave me some tissue to wipe my face and asked if I was okay. I was so happy that I started witnessing to her, telling her how good God was. I had gone from not having one dollar in my pocket a week prior and not knowing how I was going to pay my bills to being blessed with more than eight thousand dollars within three days.

Chapter Six:
Why Him?

When she was alive, it had always been a family tradition to eat Thanksgiving dinner at my aunt's house on Orange Drive. We would sit around with the newspapers from all our favorite stores and make a list of all the things we were going to buy at the after-Thanksgiving sales. After dinner, everyone would head home and get ready to get up at four o'clock in the morning. After she passed, we all decided to keep the tradition going.

Kyle didn't come with us that day. I let him sleep in and I went shopping. I always looked forward to this time of year because no matter what I was going through, the holidays always made me feel better. I didn't buy much on our shopping trip. When we were done, I headed back to the house to drop off my things and get Kyle so we could finish shopping for our children. I pulled up to the house and moved over to the passenger seat so he could drive. We had only gone three blocks from my house when my phone rang.

I kept trying to check my voicemail from my phone, but before I could, my phone died. I asked Kyle if I could use his to get a number off my voicemail. When he said yes, I picked up his phone. Before I could dial my number, I saw that he had a missed call and a text message came through. I didn't think much of it, because it had never been a problem. I handed him the phone so he could check it. When he said that it was okay and put the phone down, I got suspicious. He had never done that before. I asked him who it was and he responded, "Nobody." I asked him to check it once again but he didn't, so I took the phone and read the message. It said, "Let's make a wager. If you win, I will give you head, and if I win, you give me head." I was shocked. I didn't think I was reading it right, so I took a deep breath and told him to pull the car over. He didn't want to. Pissed, I told him, "You have two options. You can pull this car over yourself or I can pull it over for you." Knowing that I meant I would wreck it, he made the right choice and pulled over.

I sat there trying to calm down. Finally, I asked him who this person was and he claimed that she was just a friend. So I asked, "Why did she send you this message?" He said her name was Jenifer and, of course, he said he didn't know why. That's when I snatched the car keys out of the ignition and socked him in his chest so hard that he fell back into his seat. I got out of the car and started walking home. He came up behind me and tried to explain. Having nothing to lose at this point, I asked if he had slept with her. When he said he had, I slapped him in the face and his glasses fell off. He knew I was angry and I didn't care. It was not the first time I had fought a man. Keeping his distance, he just stood there while I picked up his keys. I put them in my back pocket and told him that, if he thought he was bad enough to take them, then do it. Instead, he tried to explain and tell me how sorry he was. I didn't even want to hear it. I just threw his keys down and walked back home.

When I got inside the house, I thought that I was going to be sad, but I wasn't. I just started cleaning up. After cleaning, I put on some music and took a nice, hot bath. While sitting in the bath, I started to remember a time when we were riding in the car, his phone rang, and he just hung up. When I asked who it was, he made me believe that I didn't hear it ring. So when I heard the name Jenifer, I remembered another incident when someone had called his phone, then hung up when I answered it. I called the number back and a female picked up. I asked who was she and why was she calling Kyle's phone. She tried to tell me that they worked together and they were just friends. When I confronted him about it, he said the same thing. Kyle saw how pissed I was so he called Jenifer back and said that they couldn't be friends anymore because of how upset it made me. That text meant that he had been sleeping with this girl the whole time. I was so done with him and his lies. I sat back in the tub, closed my eyes, relaxed, and tried to forget about the whole thing.

Things were pretty quiet at the house. I was finally starting to calm down when my phone rang. I didn't recognize the number, but I answered it anyway. To my surprise, it was Ms Emily, Kyle's mom. I didn't know why she was calling. Evidently, he had told her what happened and asked her to call to convince me to forgive him. She went on to tell me how sorry he was and that we all make mistakes. She proceeded to tell me about her relationships and the things that she had been through with her husband. She concluded by saying, "Look, Kyle loves you a lot. He has made some stupid mistakes, but if you give him one more chance, he promises that he will get his stuff together once and for all!" I listened to what she had to say, but I told her that I needed time to think about it and I wanted to be alone for now.

I never really could tell if Kyle's mom had good intentions, probably because she was the kind of person who didn't think about anyone but herself. Ms. Emily only did things for someone if she could benefit from it. All I could think about was how his mom and aunt would go to any lengths to pull him out of one mess or the other. No matter how wrong he was, they never let him deal with his own mistakes; they always came to his rescue. In the long run, this made life harder for him.

Once again, my mind started to drift back down memory lane. When Kyle was going through his divorce, he didn't have anywhere to live, so he went back home with his mom. The house that she lived in belonged to his grandparents. When they passed away, Kyle thought it was best to buy the house and keep it in the family. In the beginning, everyone thought this was a great idea because it kept a roof over his mom and little sister's heads. As the years went by, it became apparent that she wasn't paying any of the bills on time and was always short on the mortgage.

Eventually, he had to make a major decision that would change his family's life forever. He had to sell the family home. Before he made the decision to sell it, he desperately tried to borrow money to save it. Even though he did this, his mom still chose to spend her portion of the mortgage on clothes and vacations, instead of helping to satisfy the debt on the house. In the end, they lost the house. I will never forget the conversation they had a week before it happened.

When Kyle's wife found out the house was being sold, she did some investigating to see if she could get money from it in the divorce. She obviously was upset with him for dating me and confessed that she had always felt that his family had pulled a scam to avoid putting her name on the deed. Since he was messing around while they were still married, she decided that she would try to take whatever money they received when it was all done. At that point, his mother felt that she was justified in lashing out at him by saying, "Well, maybe you should have kept Kessan a secret and brought her around when this situation was over." Sitting there, I thought to myself, "Wow! This woman truly has two faces." That's when I knew we could never be close. I didn't trust her.

A few days before Christmas, I allowed Kyle to come over. I was on my way to take Keithshon and Jamie to get a Christmas tree. As we were walking out of the house, I got a phone call from Kyle asking what I was doing. Although I tried to be short with him, it was hard. Whenever I heard his voice, I would remember why I cared so much about him. He went on to say that he had his daughters with him. I knew that he hadn't planned to get a tree for them. I told him I would be back in thirty minutes, so if he wanted to meet me at my house that would be ok with me. When I pulled up in my truck, he was in the driveway and I told the children to get out. Before I could say anything, he was already out of his car getting the tree down and bringing it into the house. While the children were making room for the tree, I went inside and made cookies while everyone started decorating. I really didn't want him there, but I was always weak when it came to him, and it was nice to see his girls. They had become such a big part of our family. I really loved them and so did Keithshon and Jamie.

We didn't really do much for Christmas, but I cooked as always: turkey wings, a roast, candied yams, mac and cheese, green beans, and cabbage. I didn't feel like being bothered with anyone so the children and I spent some time alone and watched Christmas movies all day long. The children wanted to hang out with their friends and do something else, but I told them we were spending this time together as a family. We were going to church. Our church would be having a New Year's Eve celebration and I planned on us being there as well. I was happy about spending New Year's Eve in church. Besides, it had been a long and stressful year. I was ready for it to be over.

I could never understand why I always did this to myself. Every time I tried to push Kyle out of my life, something would pull him back in. We were getting along pretty well during and after the holidays, but it didn't take long before Kyle lied and disappeared again. I decided it was time for me to keep myself busy with work. I had recently found a job at a shoe repair shop and finally enrolled myself into Southwest

Community College. I didn't have a lot of time to think about Kyle, especially when he was tripping.

One evening in January 2007, after just finishing with my homework, I was on the phone going back and forth with Kyle. Once again, he had lied about something. Before I hung up the phone, I told him to please erase my number and never call me again. The next morning, I got in my truck, put on my favorite songs, and headed to work. I was only a block away from work when I made a right turn coming down a hill. An elderly lady stopped her car right in front of me. I couldn't hit the breaks in time and I crashed into the back of her car. She was trying a make a turn from the wrong lane which caused the crash. The next thing I knew, my air bag deployed and I was knocked unconscious.

When I woke up, I heard a man's voice asking me if I was okay. I couldn't talk. "Ma'am, do you have a cell phone," he asked persistently. I pointed to my purse on the floor and he got it out. I told him to call the last number on my phone and I didn't know at that time who he was calling. He informed the person on the other end that someone in a gray Expedition had just been involved in a bad accident and someone needed to get over to me fast. When he hung up, he explained that he had just gotten off the phone with a Kyle and he was on his way. I was relieved that this stranger stayed with me until the ambulance arrived.

I was very dizzy and my head was pounding. Once the firemen came to help me out of the truck, all I could say to myself was, "These men are so sexy and they are everywhere!" I couldn't even think straight. One was in the back seat of my truck, the others were on my left and right, and there was one inside the truck with me trying to make sure I was positioned just right so they could put me on the gurney. It just so happened that the one talking to me also knew me from the club. He told me not to worry. "You're going to be alright. I am going to take care of you." At that moment, I started to feel a little bit better even though I couldn't move. They started pulling me out of the truck and I heard someone say, "Back up. We need to get her in the ambulance!" I looked over and saw Kyle standing there. Still dazed, I didn't want to be happy to see him, but I was. At least his was a familiar face. I was terrified. As they were rolling me away,

I could see that my truck was completely totaled. Kyle followed us to the hospital and made sure he was there when they brought me into the room. He called my sister Eva, and told her about the accident and that he would stay with me until it was time for me to go home. I couldn't really walk well because my back was injured in the crash. My face was a little bruised from the airbag and I was in a lot of pain.

A little while after I was taken home, my sister came over and dropped off my medicine and a heating pad. That night, Kyle made me dinner, washed me up, and stayed with me until I fell asleep. The next morning, he even came back early just to make sure I took my pain pills and had everything I needed until he left for work. He even got mad at his sister because she wouldn't make time to come by the house to check on me throughout the day.

Kyle stayed with me day and night for the next few weeks, telling me how sorry he was and that he knew now that we were meant to be together. He reminded me that the night before the accident I told him that I was never going to talk to him again and that he knew I was done with him, especially when I didn't answer his call. When he got the phone call about the accident, he said his heart dropped after hearing a man's voice on my phone asking him if he knew anyone who drove a silver truck.

Just think, if Kyle hadn't called me that morning, his number would not have been in my phone. Too exhausted to argue, I let him talk. I really believed that he wanted to change, but deep down I knew he was far too damaged from his childhood to change. I don't remember much about his dad, except for Kyle telling me he was never faithful to any of the women he'd dated, not even his mother.

A week had passed, and I was sick and tired of sitting in the house. I needed to get out and try to walk around. I had lost my job at the shoe repair shop, so I really didn't have much money to do anything else during the day. Plus, I was stressing out because Kyle and I had been intimate the first two nights when I came home from the hospital, and we hadn't used any protection. Kyle and I went out to the park and lay around, talking and laughing. It was a beautiful day and I was enjoying his company. As I lay back on the blanket, I tried to decide what I was going to do if I really was pregnant. I didn't say anything to him, but he already knew what was on my mind. I rolled over, looked at him, and said, "So what are we going to do?" His response was, "Well, if you are, then we are just going to have to get married and make this work. Everything will be okay."

Now, the funny thing about that conversation was that even though we were talking about me being pregnant, that word never came out of our mouths. Mid-conversation I got a text message on my phone, I looked down and read it. Astonished, I dropped the phone and sat up really fast. I couldn't believe what I was reading, so I looked at the phone again and read it once more. After about five minutes of staring at my phone, I finally told Kyle, "I am about to show you something and I need you to tell me what it says." He took my phone and read the message, then looked at me and asked who'd sent it. I told him I didn't know, but how and why would this come through right now, and we had never even said the word "pregnant." I thought that maybe we were both tripping, so I tried to call the number back but no one answered. I read the text once more just to make sure and was still trying to let it sink in. It said, "Kessan, do you really think being pregnant is going to change anything?"

Neither of us could believe what we'd just read and didn't understand how it got there. After sitting there quietly for a while, I decided that it was time for me to go home. Kyle dropped me off, and I went into my house and rested the entire evening, thinking about the text message. Neither of us ever mentioned it again, even when I found out I wasn't pregnant. However, he did say the pregnancy made him want to show me that he wanted to be there for me no matter what.

Kyle decided he wanted to come to church with the children and me. He insisted on coming to pick me up. I knew that he was starting to sense that I was pulling away from him because I didn't care about him the way I use to, and I made no secret about it in my actions.

After church, I noticed this guy named Demetrius who had started coming with his parents. They were the assistant pastors at my church and he was a minister himself. After he had attended a few times, we would stand outside talking while I waited for Kyle to make his rounds and say goodbye to everyone. I didn't really find him attractive, but he was nice and we made each other laugh. We discussed the things we were currently going through. I was trying to completely walk away from my situation. He was dealing with being divorced for the past year and didn't know how to start over again. I wasn't really looking for anyone to hang out with or date, and neither was he.

Kyle's roommate, Luther, was having a birthday party on a Saturday. I had been hanging with Kyle most of the day, but I was tired and ready to go home so they could finish getting ready for the party. Kyle didn't bother to invite me, so I just went home thinking that he would call me once the party was over. When I didn't hear from him, I woke up that Sunday morning and realized I didn't have my phone charger, so I called him from my landline and asked if I had left it there. He said that I had. I told him that I was on my way to come pick it up. He told me that I didn't have to do that, and he would just meet me and bring it with him. Knowing him, that didn't seem right to me, and I told him I was on my way to come get it.

When I pulled up to the complex, I got out of the car and he was standing outside. I asked him what was going on. He tried to tell me that he didn't want me to come in because a few of Luther's female friends had spent the night, and he didn't want me to be upset. Needing to see if he was lying again, I pushed him out of my way and walked into the house. I went into his room and opened up the closet door; then I looked in the living room and didn't see anyone. Disgusted, I grabbed what I came to get and told him that I was done with him. I knew that Jenifer was in there somewhere, but I was not about to act up and be late for church, so I left.

While I was driving away, I told myself that I was done and I wasn't going back. Of course, Kyle didn't come back to church, which is what he always did when he went back to Jenifer. This time it was okay with me, I really didn't want to see him anymore and that made it a lot easier.

I started to focus more and more on school and to my surprise, Demetrius and I started talking and hanging out. We were only friends so we didn't really broadcast our friendship. We were simply enjoying each other's company. We would routinely meet up after church on the weekends. I really loved hanging out with him, and it was refreshing being around someone who was so caring. My family liked him and I noticed he liked me as well. To my surprise, one day he decided to sit next to me in church. I was nervous about this new development. He had come in during Praise and Worship, and stood in the back until it was over. After the last song, he walked toward where I was sitting and sat next to me.

Certainly, all eyes were on us. I didn't even pay it much attention because when it came to me and the church, someone was always saying something. I decided to let them talk. I enjoyed the service and sat up with my head held high. When I looked over and saw his mom, she was smiling from ear to ear. It had been her idea for us to meet in the first place. She invited me to her home one Saturday. She said she needed to talk to me about something, but I had no idea what it could be about. Little did I know that the time I spent with her would completely change my life for the better!

Demetrius picked me up early that morning because his parents lived about an hour away in Riverside. We bought coffee before getting on the road and talked the entire way there. When we arrived at his parents' home, I walked inside and his entire family was there. I guess they did this almost every weekend. I spent time with his sister and played around with his niece until his mother was ready to sit at the table to talk.

It took me a while to see where the conversation was headed, but I caught on pretty quickly as she was explaining how she saw great things in me. She had also noticed that I had let myself go a little since I'd started coming to the church. She said the first time she saw me, she knew I had something special in me. She could tell by the way I walked and talked with so much confidence. She hinted that a few folks had nasty things to say about me and my past. They even told her that I was still dipping into my old lifestyle. I was waiting for her to tell me who but she never did. She said it didn't matter. This was very upsetting, but she told me I should not worry about what people said and that God had given me many gifts. It was time to focus and seek Him more and find out what it is I was supposed to do next. She then said that I was a beautiful girl and I need not be ashamed. She told me to always walk with my head up and never let anyone make me feel bad about how God had made me, and it was time to take my place in God's kingdom.

On the ride home, I was pretty quiet. I was thinking about everything that Mrs. Phillips had said to me, and it meant the world to me. I always looked at her as a woman with a lot of class. She was very elegant and true to the meaning of a God-fearing woman. She never had anything bad to say about anyone. Instead, she would just push things aside, smile, and act as if no one had a bad bone in their body.

I remembered how confident I had been when I first came to El Shaddai. I wasn't going to allow anybody to change me or put me down. I knew that I had a body that was quite noticeable and a look that set me apart from others. But, hey, that was me! I never thought of myself as any better or any less than anyone. I just loved being happy and kind to everyone around me. I have always loved making people smile and feel good about themselves. I never thought that the people in the church would treat me the way they did. I tried to think back to when I started to let myself go. How did I allow myself to let other people's issues affect me?

Then it hit me. The first time I'd praise danced, I was in the back putting on my clothes. A sister at the church came in and asked if she could pray with me. I agreed because this person, I thought, was well respected. I closed my eyes and bowed my head. At the time, I didn't know much about praying, but I knew when someone was trying to tell you something without really saying it. She proceeded to say, "Lord, please bless this dance and allow Your will to be done. We thank You right now Lord that whatever it is in her that is not of You, we ask you to remove it now. We all thank You that she will watch her movements, and make sure that you take all that worldly stuff out of her and have your will. We thank You that she is aware of herself, and we pray that everyone out there that is skeptical about her will open up their hearts and not judge her for where she has come from."

I had one eye closed and the other open, looking at this person and thinking, *Wow, is this how others see me? I have been here a year and a half, and I didn't even want to do this dance anyway. Does she think the ex-stripper really wants to get up in front of a church and praise dance for the Lord? No! I would rather come here, get a Word that will make me a better person and be the best Christian I can be without stepping on anyone's toes, and be on my way.* I tried not to think about the prayer and tried to convince myself that she was coming from a good place. But something in my spirit wouldn't allow her words to stick, so I just said "Amen," and went out. All I wanted was to be a blessing to anyone whose heart would receive it.

Five months had passed since I'd last seen Kyle. One night I had a dream that he came back to church. I didn't know what it meant, but from past experiences with my dreams, I knew that it was God preparing me for something. I shared this dream with Demetrius because he had recently told me that he thought I had a gift from God in reference to my dreams, and that God was starting to use me through my dreams. I was still new to all of this so I just kept things to myself. I never believed I was special enough for God to use me for anything. When Kyle walked back inside the church, I just happened to turn around at the right moment. He looked at me the same way he did in my dream. It was eerie. He sat down behind me, and I turned around and didn't pay him any mind after that.

One Saturday night, Demetrius and I decided to go dinner at the Grand Lux in Beverly Hills. He had never been there, and I thought it would be nice for us to go out and have dinner. After we were seated, I ordered a cocktail and we talked for a bit. Before I could finish my sentence, I felt someone staring at me. I looked over to my right and saw Kyle's roommate. When we made eye contact, he smiled and waved, and I told Demetrious that he was there. He peered over at their table and informed me that Kyle was there too. Turning to get a better look at their group, I saw that Jenifer and his whole family were in the midst of celebrating his 33rd birthday. I thought, *What a small world!* and turned around to enjoy the rest of my evening. After we were done with dinner, we decided it was time to head out. Demetrius and I considered staying longer, but I was ready to leave and he had a long drive back home. Heading for the exit, we ran right into Kyle.

The design of the walkway made it necessary for us to pass one another in order to leave the restaurant. There was no avoiding him. Attempting to lighten the mood, Demetrius put out his hand to greet him. Kyle moved toward me in an effort to hug me, but I moved out of his way, said "Hello," and we walked away. Truly, the look on his face said it all. I had never put anyone before him and was always there to take him back whenever he was ready to act right. This time he knew it was over and I had really moved on.

That same weekend we had a second church service to attend after our regular Sunday service. The Spirit had been telling me all week that Kyle was going to bring Jenifer to church. We pulled up to the church at the same time; she was with him. With a smile on my face, Demetrius and I walked through the door. Kyle rushed over to Demetrius and introduced Jenifer as his girlfriend, but when I walked by he didn't say anything. I was praise dancing that day, so I put his craziness right out of my head. Also, I was having so much fun with my new friend Demetrius. It was like having a female best friend, only he was a guy.

Kyle started doing everything in his power to get my attention. He brought Jenifer to El Shaddai more often. No matter where I was, he made it a point to walk my way so I could see him or he could speak. I was always polite and spoke, and even made sure that I spoke to Jenifer. Frankly, I really didn't care what he was doing with his life anymore. I was happy that I had finally gotten over him and had stopped allowing him to hurt me. Actually, I felt sorry for Jenifer because everyone already knew what he was doing. Sometimes things would get awkward when he brought his daughters because they would always want to come and sit with me. Obviously, I still treated them like they were my own and it made things hard. No matter what I would say or do, Kyle could not get it through his head that I was done with him and I wasn't coming back. This fact didn't stop him from calling my sister Andrea and begging her to call and ask me to talk to him. He even came to my new job at a restaurant in Westchester to order food just so he could speak to me.

Kyle even went to Keithshon's school to attend parent-teacher conferences just so he could see me because he knew I would have to attend. I took his name off Keithshon's emergency card. When none of that worked, he had his Aunt Joan, who was more like his mother, come talk to me. "You shouldn't just walk away from what you had! He realizes that he made a big mistake leaving you and doing what he did." She even went so far as crying and begging me not to walk away from him and their family. Even though I wanted to feel some kind of emotion, something in me wouldn't allow it. I had heard this so many times before and it was always the same story. I really didn't like the fact that his aunt had come up to me and put this sad story on me right as I was leaving church. I was dealing with a lot and nobody really knew.

I was having a lot of problems with the owner of the house I was renting. I'd met her through a mutual friend and, initially, she came across as a very trustworthy person. I was tired of her being shady with the bills and rent, and although she knew that I was on a fixed income, she kept increasing the amount of money she expected from me for one reason or the other. She was already charging me more money for the house than she was supposed to. She would always say, "I'm going through some financial issues right now, so I need you just to work with me." She claimed that when she got everything together she would come down on my rent. This woman had a big, beautiful home up in the hills, drove a Mercedes, and was always throwing elaborate birthday parties for her nine-year-old son. It was hard for me to believe her stories.

When the time came for us to talk about bringing my rent down, she went off on me, acting like she'd never agreed to do so. Not only was she turning the garage behind me into a single apartment for her nephew, she wanted me to let her put the utilities onto my bill. Once I realized that she was playing games and never intended to fix the rent, I told her that I wasn't going to pay her in cash anymore. On the first day of the following month, I gave her a money order and she went off. She tried to explain to me how we had an agreement that I would only pay her in cash because she couldn't have a paper trail with the true amount I was paying her, but I didn't care anymore.

She wasn't worried about me, and for the first time, I wasn't going to worry about her. After going back and forth with my landlady, I decided that I was going to move. I hated the thought of having to do it again so soon. I had only been there two years, but I also knew that it was time for me to move on. Whenever I wasn't working, I would drive around for hours looking for a place. Everything was so expensive! I told God that if I had to move, then I wanted to move back into my old neighborhood. Three months passed and I couldn't find anything in that area, so I decided to move wherever I could.

I only had three more weeks in the house and I still hadn't found anything. One Saturday morning, I got up and looked all day. It was already seven o'clock in the evening and just as I was about to give up and go back home, I found a place that I actually liked. An apartment on Aviation and Sepulveda, close to my job on 89th and Sepulveda near LAX. I told myself that I wouldn't complain and try to be grateful for whatever He had for me at this point and time. I put in an application. I didn't hear anything right away but I had a good feeling about it.

I was at work on a Wednesday. I remember it so clearly because it was the day after our country made history by electing its first black president. Everyone was so happy. Folks were talking about the election even though we were supposed to be working; it was hard to concentrate. Many of my co-workers were taking personal calls on their cell phones, and jumping up and down to celebrate. I snuck away and went to the back to check my phone because everyone was calling and leaving messages about this landmark victory.

Right in the middle of me laughing and playing around with everyone else, my excitement changed to sadness. In between all the crazy messages, there was one from the owner of the building telling me that he was sorry but I didn't get the place. Disappointed, I slid down in a chair in the corner of the restaurant. It took me a minute to get myself together and I didn't want anyone to ask me what was wrong. I went into the restroom, called Demetrius, and told him what happened. Taking a moment to encourage me, he told me not to feel down. This just meant that God had something better for me. The Lord just had to close that door so another could be opened. That's when I told myself that I wasn't going to cry or be sad about any of this. I would just thank God for the new home that He had waiting for me, and I would keep looking.

Deciding to get an early start the next morning, I planned to go over to my old neighborhood where all my family still lived and search for my new apartment. I didn't have to work that day so I rolled myself out of the bed, made the children breakfast, hopped in the shower, and headed out for what I told myself would be a long day. I hated not having two cars to choose from any more because if there was ever a problem with one car, I could just use the other. This was one of those days. The brakes on my 1998 Ford Escort were really bad and getting louder day by day, but I wasn't going to let anything stop me from finding a place.

I'd already told myself that I wasn't going to settle for anything less than a two bedroom near my sister Eva. I wanted to move back into my old area and that's what I planned to do. I didn't look for places near my old house. Instead, I went a little further away. But for some reason, I kept getting closer to the old neighborhood in Los Angeles. I started on San Vicente and worked my way back down to Pico.

My brakes started getting worse. I thought that they were about to go out, so I did the only thing I knew to do. I pleaded with God and asked him to quiet them down until I was done looking. To my surprise, they just got louder. "Something" told me to stop by my old brake shop near Redondo and Washington Boulevard, which was right around the corner from my Aunt Bert's house where my sister lived. I really didn't want to stop there, but I had no choice.

When I pulled into the station, there was one car in front of me. I kept giving myself every excuse not to wait. Just when I was pulling off, the mechanic came running out, shouting for me to stop. "I'm ready to check your brakes," he shouted. Reluctantly, I parked the car and sat on the other side of the office waiting, but still trying to find a way to leave. I felt like I was wasting time just sitting there. I needed to be driving around looking for my new place. As I sat there, I made a few phone calls to see if the guy who worked on cars near my house was available. Of course, I couldn't find him. Then, something strange happened again. I heard a voice telling me to walk around the corner to my sister Eva's house. I really didn't want to go so I continued to sit there. Then I heard it again, "Get up and walk around the corner and pay attention." This time, I didn't hesitate. I just said, "Okay, I'm going to trust that there is something that you have for me." Puzzled but trying to be obedient to God, I started walking and looking for apartments for rent. As I reached the end of the corner, I initially didn't see anything, but as I crossed the street, I saw a sign for a two-bedroom, one-bath apartment.

I was very hesitant to call because I knew the rent would be way out my price range. I kept walking, but a voice said, "Call the number!" Without hesitating this time, I called the number and the phone only rang twice before I heard a man's voice on the other end. It caught me off guard because I thought for sure I'd get voicemail. Recovering quickly, I told him my name and the reason for my call. He explained that the place wouldn't be ready until the following month because the tenants were still there, but if I called him the next day he would try to see if they would let me do a walk through and I agreed. As I hung up the phone, I told myself that I wasn't going to waste my time. I walked around to my sister's place and waited for the mechanic to finish repairing my car.

An hour-and-a-half later, I heard the voice again say, "Go get your car, but stop back by that place and write down that number." So I did just that. While I was writing, I heard a male voice behind me say, "It's the one upstairs." When I found out that it was the same voice as the one on the phone, I asked if he was the manager. When he admitted to be the owner, I turned around and said, "Would your name happen to be Tom?" When he said it was, I explained that we had just spoken about an hour before, and we chatted for a bit. During the course of the conversation, I realized that he knew members of my family. After he heard the story as to why I had to move, he told me that if I wanted the place it was mine. No credit check or anything, just bring him some money to hold the place and I could have it. I couldn't believe what had happened. I worked overtime because I wanted to move into my new place before Christmas, which was a few weeks away. I knew this was going to be a challenge. All I had to do was come up with a few thousand to move in.

Demetrius took care of all the moving arrangements, so that was one thing I didn't have to worry about. By the grace of God, I made the deadline to leave the old house by two days. As soon as I went through the front door, I walked around the apartment and thanked God for what he had done. It was beautiful, it reminded me of a small villa in France, and I was right around the corner from my family. I thought life was pretty grand right about then. Two days before Christmas and I couldn't believe that 2008 was almost over. I had been through so much but I still had a lot to do.

I couldn't get any time off so Demetrius stayed at my new place and worked on getting the apartment together until I got home. This was very weird because we tried not to spend a lot of time together during the evening. Although we were just friends, we both knew that it was a bad idea to be alone together in the nighttime; we were both adults coming out of intimate relationships. All things considered, I figured it would be okay since he was working.

After about two weeks, things started to look quite nice. I didn't have everything I wanted in my new place, but I was happy with what I had. I was even fine with sleeping on the floor until I could afford a new bed. On the other hand, it was a different story with the children. They weren't happy and were fighting almost every morning because they went from having their own room to having to share one.

Demetrius helped a lot around the house. He would come down as much as he could to do the manly things around the house; things were looking great. We got along well, but something was missing. We talked on the phone every day, saw each other as much as we could, spent time at church together, and he even bought season passes to Magic Mountain amusement park just so we could go whenever we felt like it. I even rode with him to work while he did deliveries to the studios; at the time, he was working in the movie industry as a director's assistant.

We had a really good thing going, but we weren't getting any closer, and we both felt it. Not wanting to admit this, we decided to not talk about it and let the cards fall where they may. Unfortunately, deep down in my heart, I knew we didn't like each other in that way. It was more like a brother and sister love. No matter what, I couldn't change it. And, for the first time in my life, I didn't want a relationship.

That following week, Kyle was blowing my phone up, telling me that he needed to talk to me about something important. He was quite persistent and finally wore me down. I told him he could come by, but when he got to my place, he told me to put on something more comfortable and follow him because he needed to show me something. I was hesitant at first, but he told me that he wasn't up to anything and just needed me to come with him for a minute. He insisted that I dress in something comfortable. While following him in my car, all I could think was, *What is he up to now?* Soon, we pulled up in front of a building that ended up being a day spa. He waved his hand out the window, signaling me to park in front of him. Then he got out of his vehicle and handed me a packet. He told me to call him when I was done.

When I walked into the lobby, two women greeted me, and I handed the packet to them. I was informed that I had been given a gift certificate by Kyle for a one-hour, full-body massage. As I stood there, I wrestled with my conscious and thought, *This isn't right, I shouldn't stay. If I do, I might be sending the wrong message. Then again, it is already paid for, and it would be rude for me to just leave.* So I put my things in the locker and looked forward to my massage.

When I left, I had a message on my phone from Kyle telling me that he hoped I'd enjoyed myself. He'd just wanted to do something for me because he knew I was going through a rough patch with my children. I called him back and thanked him, but made it clear that I wasn't going to be able to accept anything like that from him again. Ignoring me, he didn't stop. Kyle knew I loved to be showered with gifts, so that's what he did. Every chance he got, he was dropping off presents at the house for me. I was determined to stop accepting things from him because I knew that if I allowed him to keep coming around, I would fall for him again. I was finally happy and I never wanted to go back to the place I always found myself in when I was with him.

Putting my foot down, I was ready for him when he made one of his unannounced "visits." I told him in no uncertain terms, no matter what he said or did, I wasn't going to take him back. Blatantly ignoring me, he kept saying, "I know you're my wife. God has been telling me this all year, and I'm finally ready to accept that." He went on to ask me if I had read the letter he'd written, declaring that we had met for a reason. He insisted that he wasn't going to give up until he got me back. At the time, I didn't care what he was saying. I told him that I was not his wife and never would be. I walked upstairs to my apartment and closed the door. I stopped taking his phone calls. I was so pissed that he would be so selfish as to try this crap again.

As time went by, he didn't stop trying, I just stopped listening! A year had already passed and I was growing further away from him. I really didn't want to deal with Kyle and his back and forth nonsense.

I was already adjusting to my feelings for Demetrius. We both knew that we couldn't use each other as a comfort zone anymore. We both wanted to be in a committed relationship one day. We had to stop acting as though we were dating, even though we were really just devoted friends. Sadly, we both decided to go our separate ways. It was hard, but we knew it was for the best. For the next couple of weeks, I kept to myself. I was sad and lonely, trying to figure out where I would go from this point on.

Folks at the church would always ask me about Demetrius, so I just told them that he was at work, which was true much of the time because he did work a lot. Everyone there had always assumed we were a couple. Honestly, I do admit to feeding into that assumption by not telling them we were just friends. I let them think what they wanted; it was my way of keeping them out of my business. Certain folks at church were always trying to find out the next big thing going on in my life. My life had become the source of juicy gossip.

Kyle was in my face every chance he had, and I already knew that he would be the first person to realize that I was no longer hanging around Demetrius. He may not have ever been good in a relationship together, but he did know me well and I knew him. I did everything I could to keep myself busy so I would not think about Demetrius. He didn't call me and I didn't call him. When we said our final goodbyes to each other, it was pretty much a wrap. I had my turbo-kickboxing class to keep my mind off what I was going through, and I was still trying to make sure that I didn't run into Kyle. We worked out at the same gym, so I would make sure I went in the evenings because he would be there in the mornings.

At church, I would leave right after service. If I stood around socializing with the members, he would attempt to make his way toward me. I really didn't need him getting into my head again. My resolve didn't last for long. One day, I was sitting on the bench at home, looking out my bay window. I was in deep thought when my phone rang. It was Kyle asking me what I was doing. Conflicted, my first mind was telling me not to reveal my true thoughts. However, my mouth won the battle, and the next thing I knew, I was telling him everything I had just gone through. Striving to be supportive, he told me that he didn't want to invade my privacy, but would I consider allowing an old friend to take me to dinner to try to make things better. Glad to get away from my dark thoughts for even just a moment, I thought, *Hey, what the heck!*

I got up, took a shower, and went out the door once I heard him pull up. I didn't know what to expect, but when it came to him surprising me, I was never disappointed. I sat back and enjoyed him treating me like a lady. Not too long afterwards, we pulled up at one of the hottest steak houses in Beverly Hills. During the meal, he tried everything in his power to get me to laugh or smile a little, but I wasn't in that kind of mood. Realizing this, he decided to turn the conversation to a more serious topic. Kyle stated that there had been something on his mind for a long time and he needed to share it with me. Striving to be courteous, I sat there listening as he started to explain that he had made a huge mistake leaving me the last time. I couldn't hide my look of irritation. Forging ahead, he told me about when he was in the bed with Jenifer and he thought he'd heard his truck starting up. He'd gone to the front window and realized that he wasn't dreaming. There were two men who had jumped-started his vehicle and they took off quickly. It was around three o'clock in the morning and he'd called the police to report it stolen. In the back of his mind, he'd heard a voice telling him that he was not supposed to be sleeping with that woman, and if he didn't stop, things were just going to get worse. According to him, that was when it hit him that his life was with me, not with her. In order to get his attention, God allowed his truck to be stolen. Nothing he was saying made any sense to me. I was thinking this was another one of Kyle's ploys to work on my weaknesses, so I changed the subject and concentrated on my great meal.

Another year had passed and our annual women's church conference was coming soon, and I was so ready to get away. I was on the program to give a praise dance and lead the workout class for the two days we would be there. This was just what I needed to boost my morale, so I was very excited. It was my chance to get away from everything that I was dealing with for little while.

When I went over to the church for the meeting to discuss our duties for the week, a sister stood up and announced that we were going to need some men of valor to come down with us so they could help with the heavy lifting. My first impression was that there would be married men coming down because they had never allowed the single brothers to come to the conference before. However, when I got home, I received a phone call from Kyle saying that he needed to let me know that he was one of the men chosen to go. I almost dropped my phone. I didn't know what to say. Endeavoring to keep my composure, I said, "Well, I guess I will see you there." Using this opportunity to his advantage, he asked if I wanted to ride to the conference with him. Giving it a few seconds of thought, I told him that I would get back to him with my decision. Realizing this wouldn't be a good idea, I called him back and told him that I would see him there.

I ended up riding down to the conference with Lashawn and a few other young female congregants from our church. Lashawn was chaperoning these young ladies who were troubled and needed this experience. They didn't have the money to pay the expenses of the conference, so she and her husband had paid their way. Wisely, Lashawn had also offered to stay in the room with them. Once we arrived at the hotel, we put our bags down, unpacked what we required for the moment, took a shower, and got dressed. Every year, there was a theme for each night. The first night's theme was "Girls Rock." As expected, we had to dress the part.

Kyle arrived a few hours after me. When I saw him come in, I must admit I was kind of happy, but couldn't explain why. Already busy helping our First Lady, Sister White, I couldn't greet him while he was bringing in some of the musical equipment for the following day. Waving as we passed by one another, we both attended to our appointed tasks and left it at that. After everyone else left to go to their rooms and get some rest, I had to stay downstairs to pray and listen to the song that I had chosen as the piece to minister in dance for the attendees. In addition, I had to get the workout routine together and be ready to MC the next day. I had a lot on my plate. Anything that would keep my mind off Kyle was fine with me.

I woke up early the next morning, eager to get my day started. As I was walking out of my room to head downstairs, who do I see coming out his room? Kyle, of course! Watching him walk toward me, I found myself getting nervous and excited all at the same time. When he caught up with me, he put his arm around my waist and gave me a big hug. Headed to the gym to exercise before the festivities began, he said he was coming to see if I was going to the gym before I taught my workout class. I wanted to hug him back, but I kept my composure. Confused, I didn't really know if I missed him or was I just desperately lonely since Demetrius was no longer around for me to talk to. After I told him I was indeed on my way there, he asked if he could tag along. Not seeing any harm in his request, I assured him it was fine.

After I taught the class, I went back to my hotel room and took a shower. Later, as I was leaving, Kyle was waiting for me. As we walked out, I noticed that all eyes were on us. Sure that they were dying to know the four-one-one, I tried to stay away from him the rest of the day. Somehow, he managed to be seated at the same table with my sisters, Angie and Andrea, and me. During the break before the next service, he even walked over to the nearby shopping mall with me. Yes, he charmed me into allowing him to buy me a few things. Kyle was a pro at getting my attention. Working our way back to the hotel, I marveled at how I had forgotten just how easy it was to be around him and how good our conversations usually were. But I knew for sure that I wasn't ready to let him back in.

As Mistress of Ceremonies for the first service on Friday morning, I had to arrive early, ready to usher in the praise and have a good time doing so. Operating in my purpose, I went over to the conference room to set up in plenty of time before the service began. The speaker for this day was a very powerful woman named Minister Terry. This lady was raised with the Word, street smart, and straight to the point about everything. She knew how to get in your face and let you have it, but make you feel loved at the same time. She was good! The first time I'd heard her preach was at the very first conference I had attended. In fact, she was the very same minister who had given me the Word that I was going to minster to girls in alternative lifestyles by witnessing and helping them gather the strength to stop dancing for money. Furthermore, I was destined to have a strong and powerful praise dance ministry. Truly, everything she said had come to pass. Needless to say, I was looking forward to the Word she was going to bring forth that day.

Every time I went up to speak, I saw Kyle standing in the back of the room watching my every move. Trying hard to stay focused, I turned in a direction so I wouldn't be able to see him anymore. But every time I looked around, he was right there offering water and making sure I had everything I needed.

Once the afternoon service concluded, all I wanted to do was eat lunch and take a nap. I wanted to rest before the evening service, so I went back to my room, turned off my cell and went to sleep. At ten minutes to six, my alarm went off and woke me up. Still feeling tired, I knew I could easily sleep for three more hours, but I knew I was needed downstairs. I rolled over, hit the alarm, put on a robe, and ran to the bathroom to get into the shower. I drank some tea, since I wouldn't be able to eat until after the dance. Refreshed, I grabbed my earphones and went down to the lobby to sit and pray until it was time for me to go on.

Lashawn was downstairs waiting for me as usual; she was my armor bearer. This is someone who makes sure you have everything you need before, during, and after preaching or performing. If there was something missing, she would go find it. Lashawn always helped me get dressed and prayed with me before I went on, stood by my side until I went out, and was waiting when I returned. I have never known what a true friendship looked like until I met her.

Kyle was also standing with me, making sure that my music was up front and my water was at the door, so when I came back from dancing he was right there. Now, Lashawn never cared for Kyle much because she was always the one helping me up when he was knocking me down. Whenever we were all at church together, everyone usually put their differences aside to focus on what was important—fellowship! But she was still human and my dear friend, so that never stopped her from letting him know that she was watching him and was up on his game when it came to me. When it was time for me to go out, I said my last prayer and stood before the congregation. I have to admit that I was a little nervous because the song I was ministering to was a little different from the ones I was used to. Determined to put myself in an atmosphere of praise, I allowed the Lord to use me the way He always did.

When I started to dance, I looked out at the people to get their attention. I began slowly, letting the Holy Spirit take its rightful place inside my being and transform me into a vessel of praise. Just when I thought this dance would be just like all the rest, the power of the Lord descended down upon the room. People started getting up, shouting, praising and crying. When the dance was over, there wasn't a dry eye there.

As I walked out to the hallway to catch my breath, I found Lashawn right beside me, handing me water and checking to make sure I was alright. Before I could catch my breath, a woman came outside and hugged me. She was crying and telling me how blessed she was by the dance. Deeply moved, I wanted to pray with her but I was still recovering from the move of God during my dance. As if on key, Lashawn took her by the hand, walked her over to the other end of the room, and prayed with her, which gave me the chance to sit down in the first chair I saw. I really needed time to collect myself and come back from the spiritual high I was on. Closing my eyes, I tried to relax but as soon as I covered my face with my hands, I felt a hand on my shoulder telling me what a wonderful job I had done.

I tried to stay away from Kyle for the rest of the conference. Everywhere I went, he was nearby. It got to the point that I started not to care how close he was. When it came time to pack up, get on the road, and head home, I put all my things in the car and told him that I was going to ride home with my sister Christina since she and I really didn't get to spend much time together at the conference. I told him that I would see him when he got back. On the ride back, all I did was chide myself for allowing him in my space over the weekend. That was not supposed to happen. Right then and there, I promised myself that I would never let him back into my personal space ever again. I vowed that I would always stay in control when it came to him.

After the two-and-half-hour drive home, my sister Christina dropped me off. I went back out to the store and bought myself a steak to cook for dinner. I was so tired from the festivities of the weekend that all I wanted to do was find a good movie on television, turn my phone off, lay on my couch, and rest for the next two days. Just as I was dozing off to sleep, I got a text from Kyle asking if I had made it home okay. I'm guessing that when I thought I'd turned the phone off, it had inadvertently gone to silent mode instead. Feeling safe enough to do so, I responded by telling him that I did. He asked if he could come over for a while because he was in the neighborhood. My first inclination was to refuse, but something deep inside me wanted to see him. I texted him and gave my consent. It seemed he was only around the corner and wasn't telling a lie; he pulled up in less than ten minutes. As he was climbing up the stairs, I found myself just staring at him. This was crazy, right? We had just spent an entire weekend together but I was still secretly happy to spend a little more time with him.

We chatted about the conference and expressed how much we both enjoyed it. Kyle went out of his way to tell me how much he was blessed when I praise danced. He said that I was a tremendous blessing to everyone present, and he always loved watching me, which was one of the things I used to love about him. He always knew how to motivate me. In the past, I had hung on every word he said until I learned how to motivate myself. At the same time, he still had a way of saying things that made me feel valued, and I think that was a big part of our relationship for a long time. For the next few weeks, he and I started spending more and more time together. We would go out to eat, went for walks, and even scheduled activities together with our children.

For some reason that I could not begin to fathom, I started to see a change in him and a part of me wanted to know if what I saw was real. Every chance he got, he would let me know how happy he was to be back in my life. He promised me that if I gave him another chance, there would be no need for us to do the dating thing, we would just straight into marriage. He said over and over that we already knew everything we needed to know about each other, and it wouldn't make any sense to date. Kyle was waiting patiently for me to say those magic words and tell him that I was ready to take one last chance with him and go all the way. Even though what Kyle was saying made me want to run away, in the back of my mind I knew I wanted a man to choose me to be his wife. That's what I thought was missing in my life, that I wouldn't feel complete until I could be called Mrs. Someone. Seriously, I didn't think I would ever have the guts to say those words to him. True, a part of me still loved him, but every time I thought about being with him in that way, all I wanted to do was run. I would just smile and avoid the subject all together.

Kyle and I started spending more time together than I really thought was wise. I knew the more time I spent with him, the more my heart would open up to him. After a while, I let my guard down and didn't want to push him away. Things seemed to feel right in a rather weird way. I didn't really have any bad feelings toward him anymore because I had forgiven him for the things he'd done in the past. Thinking positively, I was trying to focus on the new man I was dealing with.

I hadn't been to Kyle's house in a very long while, so when he invited me over to have dinner, chill, and hang with him and the girls, I thought, *Why not? It wasn't like I had plans.* When I got there, we sat down and ate dinner, then watched television while he folded up his clothes. After a few hours had passed, I started getting sleepy and told him I was going to call it a night and head home. I knew that he didn't want me to go and was probably hoping that I would stay the night. I was nowhere near ready to think about that, let alone stay the night. With a sigh, he put on his shoes, which were always by the front door, and walked me to my car. Not ready to end the evening, we walked slowly, enjoying the night air, laughing and talking about life until we finally got to the car.

He opened the door for me and gave me a nice goodnight hug. As he was stepping back, his face was close to mine, and when I looked up at him, I knew it was coming. We moved in toward each other and kissed, a very long, passionate lip-lock, knowing it wasn't the best idea. Caught up in the moment, I still let myself fall into his arms. His hands wrapped around my waist as he pulled me in so close my body became a part of his. When we first embraced, my arms were hanging down by my side, but the longer we kissed the weaker I became. I wrapped my arms around his waist, drinking in the moment. Out of breath, we pulled away, and I hurried up and said goodbye, got in the car, and drove away before anything else could be said. As usual, he yelled out, "Call me when you get home!" I stretched one arm out the window to let him know I'd heard him and I would call.

On my way home, I wouldn't allow myself to think about the kiss. I realized that something had happened that I couldn't take back or just act like it hadn't occurred at all. Safely back at home, I sent him a text to let him know that I had made it in one piece. Calling him might open the door to a conversation that I wasn't ready to have. By the time he responded, I had taken my shower, said my prayers, and gone to bed.

A few weeks later, we were hanging together like old times. He even stayed the night after taking me to dinner one Sunday night. The next morning, I woke him up early and told him that he should go home because I had to get ready for school. Since I'd moved back on the Westside, I'd checked out of Southwest College, enrolled in Santa Monica, and decided to finish up there. Instead of just letting me get up and get ready, he reached over, grabbed me, and started to tickle me. After I got out of his grip, he jumped up, said he was taking me to school, and coming back to pick me up. He had something important to do that day, so he was going to take the day off, and we could spend time together after I left school.

I was happy when I saw him waiting for me after class. I hopped into the truck; the first thing he did was reach over and gave me a big kiss right on the lips. We headed down to Melrose to get something to eat; after that, we just rode around. We hung out at the mall and later went to Trader Joe's down the street off La Brea. We decided to do a little bit more grocery shopping after Trader Joe's, so we went across the street to Ralph's to finish shopping. I got out in front and he drove into a parking space. When he parked his truck, for some reason I looked over my shoulder at the truck, and I saw something, but didn't know what it was. So I just left it alone and waited for him to catch up with me. We rushed to do the shopping because I wanted to hurry up and get home to start cooking and finish cleaning up my house. I figured we were only in the store for about thirty minutes. When we walked outside, Kyle was pushing the basket and I was telling him a joke about the woman in front of us who kept making goo-goo eyes at him.

As I was walking in the general direction where he parked the truck, I didn't see it at first and thought, *Wait a minute. We must be on the wrong row because I don't see the truck.* We walked a little further and I began to feel a nasty dread creeping into my heart. Right then, I said, "Please, Lord, no! Don't tell me that they stole his truck again in broad daylight after he just got it out the shop three weeks ago."

We walked down to where he'd parked his truck to confirm that it really was gone. I put my hand over my mouth and said a prayer. After the police came and took his statement, my sister Eva came and picked us up. The ride to my house was made in complete silence. All I could think about was that maybe this was a sign that we weren't supposed to be together. After I made sure he was okay, I fully intended to back away from him.

Shortly thereafter, we pulled up into my driveway and I picked up my car. Wanting to be helpful, I asked if he wanted to ride around and try to look for his truck. He declined my offer; he said he was hungry and needed to get something in his stomach. Hoping that would cheer him up a little, we drove over to an Italian restaurant that we liked and sat in silence. In an effort to show my support, I said, "Don't worry about it. We will get through this together. If you need to use my car for a few days, that would be fine.

Before I could continue speaking, he stopped me and replied, "I have to tell you something. I woke up this morning and wanted to ask you an important question, but my spirit told me to wait. When I heard the Spirit, I didn't know why or what I was waiting for; but now I know I've been waiting for you to say what you just said. Now, I know why my car was stolen. It all happened for a reason." That's when he said it, "Kessan Mandolph, will you marry me?"

Chapter Seven:
The Completion

As I was lying in bed thinking about what had happened the day before, I couldn't help but think, *What the heck did I just do? Did I really just say 'Yes' to him? To Us? Why did I do this? Well, there's no turning back now, so I guess the next thing to do is to meet with Pastor White and go through a few months of counseling.* Our pastor had a policy that before he would agree to marry a couple, they must go through premarital counseling.

I kept trying to push the date off to meet with Pastor so Kyle took it upon himself to set it up for us. We talked with Pastor and he agreed to do the ceremony. I kept thinking that I wasn't ready to do this. I went back and forth with myself, thinking about the prospect of spending the rest of my life with this man even though I wasn't truly in love with him. Maybe this was how it was supposed to be? Maybe leaving him and making him suffer allowed him to realize that he had a good thing. And, just maybe, he was ready to get himself together and do the right thing with me. Still, after going over this dilemma in my mind constantly, something still wasn't sitting right in my spirit.

Kyle and I could not agree on a wedding date. I wanted to wait for a while, until the following year. But he kept insisting that we needed to do it now. His argument was, "Why are we waiting? We have already been through the good and bad, and we should just start our lives as a married couple." Finally, I agreed and told him that he could pick a date, but when he said February 14, 2010, I said, "No, not going to happen!" Not to be put off easily, he said, "Fine, let's just go for December 5, 2009." This was only a month away; I was not pleased but I agreed.

A week before the wedding, everyone was excited but me. Actually, I was more focused on school than anything because I had finals all that week. I already had my dress and shoes, the only thing we hadn't done was pick out the ring. Yes, I thought it was unusual, but our finances were really bad at the time. This part was easy and we both totally agreed on this one thing: we would find something cheap and buy a nice one later.

The night before the wedding, my house was filled to the rafters with people. My sisters were in the kitchen cooking, children were running around the living room, and my nieces were sitting out on the front porch catching up on old times. Kyle was at his house with all of his boys; they wanted to give him a bachelor party, but he quickly declined. Instead, he wanted us to go up to the club where I use to work. That was where we'd first met, and it would be a great way to close out one chapter of our lives and get ready to open a new one.

At first, I didn't want to go out, but everyone pushed me to go out and enjoy my last night as a single woman. When I walked into The Blue Room, my old boss was sitting in his favorite spot at the end of the bar. He was surprised to see me; he never thought that I'd step foot back in there. I explained to him that I was about to get married and wanted to see a few of the girls. He congratulated Kyle and me, and said that the drinks were on him; he also said that he was happy for us. Kyle and I sat at a table in the corner while a few of my old co-workers came over to us and talked. We were only there for two hours before I said that I was ready to go. I didn't feel the same being there; it made me uncomfortable and sad. I couldn't stand to see girls I cared about having to deal with the mess and drama that still hovered over the club. I could sense from the ones who came to sit next to me to talk that they didn't want to live the lifestyle anymore. They just didn't have a clue on how to walk away from it all; I understood and felt their struggle.

I didn't have much to drink that night out before the wedding because I didn't want a hangover the next morning. Kyle was supposed to go and spend the night at a friend's place. We got in so late that he stayed the rest of the night with me, but I made sure he got up early the next day to get himself together. Lashawn got to my house around nine o'clock. She wanted us to go get a good work out before the wedding. She also figured this would stretch me out because she knew that Kyle and I hadn't been together for at least a year. For that matter, I hadn't been sexually active in a while. Doing what only a true friend would do, she took me over to the yoga room and made me get into yoga positions that would have me sore for weeks afterwards. We couldn't really workout long, time was running out and we still needed to get home to eat a little something, get our manicures/pedicures, then dash back home to get my makeup done.

With time winding down, I still didn't feel the shiver of excitement that a bride should feel on her wedding day. As I sat and got pampered, I listened to the "oohs" and "ahhhs" coming from friends and family, and I finally said to myself, "Wow! I'm about to get married." When I got up to put on my dress, I had one person doing my hair, the other putting on my shoes, and everyone else was in the other room yelling that it was time to go. Anxiously, I started to get butterflies right in the middle of my stomach. For the first time since all this marriage stuff had happened, I actually had happy thoughts about my new life.

While everyone else was still trying to get themselves together, Lashawn and I were rushing out the door to head over to the church. The 10 freeway was a little crowded and I knew we were going to be late. It didn't seem to bother me much. Once we arrived, we parked in front of El Shaddai. My wedding coordinator Sister Rose, who is also my prayer partner, was standing in front waiting to rush me to the back so no one would see me.

My wedding was supposed to start at three p.m. It was already three-fifteen. Lashawn left me alone for a while to go into Pastor White's office to sign the marriage license where Kyle and our other witness were waiting. I sat alone with my thoughts. Just as I started to question myself about what I was about to do, the door opened and I was told it was time to begin the ceremony. I picked up my bouquet and got in position to walk down the aisle. I couldn't see what was going on inside the church because I was standing behind the wall of the church, waiting for my cue. When I heard the song *All My Life* by Jodeci end, I took a deep breath, and I heard my song begin. That was my signal, so I proceeded to march out from behind the wall. As I appeared, the guests stood up. They were smiling and taking pictures. I had officially become a blushing bride. In that beautiful moment, I felt like I had made it to the point in my life that I thought would make me complete. I had been chosen. I had been someone's baby's mama for years. Now, it was my turn to be someone's wife.

Although I had been through this before, this time was special. I was getting married in God's house. My pastor and spiritual father was giving me away. I felt so loved. This was the type of love that I had wanted and needed for such a long time. Someone actually wanted me. Someone needed me in their life and wanted to spend the rest of their time and space with me. When I was very young, I never imagined someone like me being put on a pedestal by anyone, and now it was finally my turn.

I tried not to look anyone in the eye so I turned to my right and focused all my attention on Kyle. All I could think was, *Wow! He looks good and I can't believe that we are really here after everything we have been through.* All the fighting, crying, and screaming had finally paid off. I had won! God was finally giving me what I wanted. It had to be true or else the Lord would not have allowed him to come back into my life. He had gone from being this wandering man to one who had been spending all his time with me for the last few months. I was now at the altar, standing in front of the man I loved. Kyle and I stood staring into each other eyes, waiting for the most important words we had longed to hear for the past five years.

So, after all the blah blah blah, it was finally time for, "I now pronounce you husband and wife. You may now kiss your bride!" And boy did we kiss! We didn't leave the church right away. Everyone stayed after the ceremony and had cake. A few people said some very encouraging words, and a few said some things to help us remember how far we'd truly come. Jamie even stood up with tears in her eyes, expressing how happy she was to finally have a father figure in her life, and she couldn't wait for her brother to come home from jail so we could be a family. She expressed that she knew how hard it had been for me when Keithshon had gone to jail for stealing, and I hadn't seemed happy in a long time. She said for the first time in a long time, I had a smile in my heart and that was what I deserved.

After we left the church, Kyle and I, along with a few friends, went out to dinner. His mother, Ms. Emily, and sister, Myeshia, were also in attendance. We didn't have the money for a reception, but my eldest sister was throwing a Christmas party for her union and turned her party into a celebration for us. It was perfect! She announced to the crowd that this was our wedding day. They allowed us to have our first dance and even had a photographer there who took our wedding picture. It was a wonderful day. I couldn't have planned it any better if I had done it myself.

It was getting late and we were both ready to go home and spend some time alone. He was quite nervous; it was like it was our first time. When we walked into the house, I went straight to the bedroom and he went to the bathroom. I didn't know if he wasn't feeling well because of all the excitement or if he was just as scared as I was. I didn't buy anything new to wear. Instead, I found an old, sexy nightgown that I had never worn for him. I turned on some soft music and sat on the bed waiting for my new husband.

When I heard the bathroom door open, the butterflies went crazy inside my stomach. I tried to be sexy but for some odd reason everything I knew just went out the window. When he entered the room, he had this big smile on his face. He kissed me very softly and laid me on the bed; then we made love for the first time as husband and wife. I thought that we were going to sleep in, but we both woke up early enough to make it to church. When we walked in, everyone greeted us as we took our seats and received a powerful Word from Pastor White. After service was over, we went out to eat before we went to pick up Jamie. Of course, we made a pit stop at home for some alone time. We were newlyweds after all.

I was still in school, so come Monday morning I picked up my life as a student, right where I'd left it on Friday. I never thought it was a good idea to have a wedding right in the middle of finals, but I figured if it was meant to be that everything would fall in place. Monday morning came and we both got up around five-thirty a.m. to go to the gym and work out. Before we were married, Kyle told me about all of these plans he had for us, like working out every morning together and saving our money so by the next year we could have most or all of our debt paid off. We also wanted to have enough money to move into a larger place since we had a large family with my two children and his two. We were all living in a two-bedroom apartment. Although we only had his girls on the weekend, we knew that eventually they were going to need their own room.

We didn't get to work out long at the gym that morning because we got a late start. We would usually get to the gym around five a.m., but that morning we got there at five-forty-five, so we were only able to work out for an hour. He had to get to work and I needed to head to class. I still needed to get home to make his breakfast and lunch for work. For the first two weeks, things were really hard. I felt as if I couldn't do it. I guess I hadn't really thought this whole thing out. I knew I could be a good wife because I loved to cook and take care of my man. I loved being a mother and taking care of my children, but I had no idea what I had gotten myself into combining them both.

In the beginning, we had the girls every other weekend, but their mother, Britney, thought it wasn't enough. Their time went from every other weekend to every Friday, Saturday, and every other Sunday. My life went from crazy to way out of control. Kyle eventually started getting stressed out and was really quiet a great deal of the time. No matter what I said or did, I couldn't get him to talk to me. Finally, one night we sat down together. He explained that his ex-wife Lacey was not happy with their arrangement, and she needed six hundred dollars a month for the girls. We also had to pick the girls up every day after school, help them with their homework, feed them dinner, and keep them until it was time for them to go home at six-thirty p.m. Additionally, we had them every Friday, Saturday until noon, and every other Sunday. I thought that was a bit much, but I decided I needed to step back and let him take care of things.

Things were disorganized in our household for a while, but somehow we found a way to make things work and enjoy the holidays. We spent Thanksgiving with my family, and we agreed to spend Christmas with his mom and sister. Early Christmas morning, Kyle dropped the children off with their mother and came back to the house. We had promised Ms. Emily that we would bring a dish, so Kyle thought it would be fun for us to make some mac and cheese together. I was truly falling in love with this new man. Every time I turned around, I would catch him looking at me. He would come up behind me and kiss me just because. He would look me straight in my eyes and tell me that I made him very happy. We were so caught up in these moments with one another that time flew by faster than we intended. We took a shower and drove over to the eastside to pick up his daughters, then headed out to his mother's house in Pasadena.

I wasn't happy about spending Christmas with his mom, but I knew it wasn't just about me anymore. I had to learn to like her, although this was very hard. In the weeks prior, she'd been arguing with Kyle and had said she wasn't coming to the wedding. Somehow, she didn't think it was fair to Jenifer. I couldn't understand that. She knew that Jenifer was the woman who her son had cheated on me with for years. She once claimed that she didn't care for Jenifer. Now her story was different. I had never really liked Ms. Emily and had always felt that she wasn't a good mother. All of Kyle's issues stemmed from her bad parenting. All she ever thought about in most situations was how she could benefit, but it was time to try to put all this behind me since she was now my new mother-in-law.

We arrived at her house just in time to have dinner. I went into the kitchen to see if I could help with anything, but she already had everything out and ready to go. While she and Kyle sat and talked for a minute, I went into the other room to greet his sister. She was pregnant with her second child and was really sick. I talked and joked with her, and tried to make her feel better. Unfortunately, she just wasn't feeling up to being playful. Myeshia and I had a pretty good relationship; I guess she'd always looked at me like the big sister she'd never had. When it was time to eat, everyone went into the dining room, said a prayer over the food, and we dug in. One thing I can say about his mom is that she knew how to cook a great meal, which was always a plus.

There wasn't much to do after dinner, so Jamie and I sat in the living room, watched the Lakers game, and relaxed until it was time to go. Even though I hadn't thought I would have a good time there, it turned out better than I had expected. It was getting late, so we said our goodbyes. After putting the girls in the car, we decided that we would drop them off at their mom's house instead of having them spend the night. His youngest daughter, Sidny, had been crying all day for her mother, and kept asking if she could go home to see her. Seeing how very upset she was, Kyle called their mother on the way home so he could ask her if we could drop them off over there.

Imagine our surprise when she refused. In response, both of the girls started crying hysterically and wouldn't stop. They kept asking her repeatedly, "Mommy, why? I want to come and see you." But she wouldn't change her mind. Upset by their obvious distress, I told their dad to bring them home with us. When we got into the house, I had the worst headache. Sidny cried all the way home. She kept asking Kyle why her mom wouldn't allow them to come home, and saying that she was missing her very much. Once we got into the house, I ran them a bath, dressed them for bed, and held Sidny in my arms almost all night, rocking her and telling her that she would see mommy in the morning. She finally fell asleep, with Kylia lying at the end of the bed watching cartoons.

That night I lay in bed trying to figure things out. Britney was a good mom, so I couldn't help but think something more was going on than what Kyle was telling me. It was strange that she did not want to see her girls. For the moment, I decided to leave it alone. I closed my eyes and the next thing I knew it was morning. I woke up to a little munchkin playing with my hair. She was laughing and saying, "Kessan, Kessan, I'm hungry!" I opened up one eye and saw Sidny sitting up, smiling. I grabbed her, put her on the other side of me in the bed, and tickled her until she couldn't take it anymore. I asked her where her sister was. She said that Kylia was in the bed with Jamie, and daddy was on the computer. So I got myself out of bed, kissed my husband on the forehead, and started making breakfast.

Once we had eaten, everyone sat around watching television. I knew that we were going to take the girls home later that afternoon. I tried to relax before I had to comb the girls' hair and get them dressed. This whole process always threw me for a loop because my children were teenagers and I hadn't had to get children dressed or do a child's hair in years. It really didn't help matters that they were five and six years old, respectively, with thick, long hair, not to mention that they were both very tender-headed.

When Kyle got home from dropping the girls off, he was a little upset so I didn't bother him. I just waited to see what he would do next. Much later, I overheard him on the phone in the bedroom talking with the girls' mother. He was extremely angry and yelling into the receiver. I went into the bedroom after he'd hung up to see what had brought on the argument. He explained that when he'd dropped the girls off at home, Lacey wanted to know when he would start to give her the extra money. She told him that she had bills to pay and things to do for the girls.

Now, I didn't understand any of this. How could Britney want more money for the girls when she didn't have them that much? When they went home in the evening, all she had to do for them was give them a bath and put them to bed, and they did most of that on their own. I really didn't understand where all this need for extra money was coming from. Kyle promised to go over there after church on Sunday to meet with her and her mom to try to work out some sort of agreement with them.

After church, Kyle dropped me off at home and headed over for his meeting. At first, I was upset but I knew I couldn't say much. I kept thinking about how hard things were for us at the time. Additionally, we hadn't had much alone time since we'd been married, and everything was moving so fast. I resented the fact that he was allowing her to run my home. The more I thought about it, the angrier I became. To take my mind off the whole mess, I started dinner and tried to do some homework.

It was around five-thirty when Kyle got back home. As soon as he came in the door, I asked what happened. He then told me that he had agreed to give her two hundred dollars extra per month, and he would buy their uniforms, socks and underwear. Taken aback, I thought about what she was doing and wondered why all of a sudden, right after we got married, did she start making all these demands. Fed up, I put my foot down and told him that this wasn't going to work and it wasn't fair to me. I had papers to write, dinner to cook every night, and two children that I was taking care of. Why was it o.k. for her to have all this freedom and not have to help with her own children? I really didn't understand why he was allowing her to have her way like this. She was getting everything she asked for, but when I said anything, he would just tell me to let him handle it. He promised it would be o.k. It was not o.k. that he'd agreed to give her more money without discussing it with me first.

I knew that it was time to have a serious talk. I had been the good, quiet wife for long enough. It was bad enough that we were going through this, but when my car broke down on the freeway the next day, I felt that I had taken more than my share. After dropping Kyle off, something in my soul told me to check his phone. But when I asked him for it, he gave me this look as though he didn't want to give it to me. I just shook it off as I had done everything else those days.

As I was heading to school, my car started to smoke and kept trying to cut off in the middle of morning traffic. I got all the way over to the right-hand lane, and as soon as I got to an open spot, my car stopped. Trying to stay cool, I sat there fighting to calm down and think this thing over. This couldn't be happening right now! I had a test in my History class that I couldn't miss. Stressed out, I took a deep breath, called Kyle at work, and told him what happened. He told me to call AAA and have the car towed to the house. We were experiencing drama on every hand.

Over the next few weeks, things were not very good between us. Kyle would get up and go to the gym at five in the morning without me, and when he came back home, he would get in the shower and get ready for work without even saying two words to me. He didn't even come directly home anymore. Since he had his aunt's car, he would drive her around to help her take care of her business. We had a few disagreements that he didn't even try to work out. Instead, he just got up and left.

I remember one night Lashawn was having a get-together for her married friends. She had a woman come to her house to host a Pure Passion toy party and show us gifts we could buy that would add excitement to our marriage. Before I left to go over to Lashawn's place, I told Kyle that I was going to need to take the cell phone with me because we only had one at the time. We had been sharing it for the last few months, until he could buy me a new one. When he turned to me and asked, "For what?" I immediately became suspicious. He already knew that most of my insecurities in the past had stemmed from him and that phone. That's how I would always know he was messing around with Jenifer. I looked at him in disbelief and asked him why it was a problem. After all, he knew it was late at night, I was driving all the way to Long Beach alone, and I always got lost. Then I said, "And by the way, why are you tripping about me taking the phone anyway? It has never been a problem." When he saw how angry I was getting, he told me to take the phone and that he was sorry for overreacting. Still a little suspicious, I wanted to question him more, but I didn't have the time and I was tired of fighting so I just gave him a kiss and left.

I couldn't really enjoy myself at the party. Instead, I kept looking at my phone to see why Kyle hadn't called to see if I made it safely. When it did ring and I saw it was the house number, I felt much better. I answered and was expecting to hear his voice, but it wasn't him. It was my daughter Jamie asking me where I'd put her clothes after I took them out the dryer. After I told her that they were in her dresser where they belonged, I asked her where Kyle was. Jamie told me that he was in the bedroom sleeping. After I hung up the phone, I knew it was time for me to go home. I had only been there a few hours, but after that phone call, I couldn't really focus or have fun. I got up to leave, said goodbye to everyone, and headed home.

When I got home, I went into the room and Kyle was fast asleep. I sat on the bed next him and told him to wake up because we needed to talk. After a few seconds, he rolled over and opened his eyes, but didn't say much. Getting straight to the point, I asked him what was going on and how did we end up in this place? He tried to act as if he didn't have a clue to what I was referring. Then I asked him why he hadn't bothered to call me to see if I had made it to Lashawn's house okay, and when I would be home. He looked at me and admitted, "I was mad when you left the house. I didn't understand why you were tripping over the phone." He added that I had been acting funny lately as well.

When he said that, I lost it and let everything that was bothering me spill out. I proceeded to remind him that a few nights ago when we were in the car, he'd told me that I wasn't supporting him with this situation with Britney, and to be patient because he had everything under control and things would work out. I reminded him that I had his back and trusted him, but I'd had asked him to do me one favor and just make her take the girls every other weekend so that we could have some time to ourselves. We were newlyweds and we hadn't had much alone time. All he could say to me was, "I hear what you're saying," adding that I was not going to tell him what to do.

I sat there crying and explaining, "I am your wife and you're making sure Britney is happy, but you're not even trying to make sure I'm okay. I still can't believe while we were talking you just get out of the car and come into the house. Now you're just lying in the bed while I'm trying to talk to you, and the only thing you can say is, 'You are mad at me for taking your phone?' There is definitely something else going on and I need you to tell me what it is!"

At that point, he got up from the bed, sat on the edge of it, and said, "I can't be here right now." He needed to leave and clear his head. When he got up at twelve o'clock at night and put on his clothes, I grabbed my Bible and started reading it aloud. I didn't know why I was doing it but I knew that was all I could do. I didn't want to fuss or fight because I was hurting on the inside. I needed to cry, but something wouldn't let me do it. I just kept reading. For a moment, he stopped and stood still until I was done. When I put the Bible down, he grabbed his keys and left. I didn't ask where he was going or when he was coming back. I just lay down on my bed and went to sleep.

A few hours later, I heard our bedroom door open as I looked at the clock; it read three-fifteen a.m. I didn't even roll over to say anything to him as he took off his clothes and climbed into the bed. He moved close to me and wrapped his arm around me. He told me how sorry he was for not calling and checking on me. He wanted to know all about the party and if I brought anything home with me. I rolled over to face him, looked him in his eyes, and said it was okay; we would talk about it in the morning. As I rolled back over, he wrapped his arms tightly around me and we fell asleep.

Kyle didn't work out the next morning; he slept in instead. I didn't sleep very well because of the argument the night before, but I figured I would just let it go because he did come back home, and all married people go through their ups and downs. We just so happened to be going through a down stage after being married for only a month. I already knew that things weren't going to be perfect and that marriage would be a lot of work, but when I decided to say, "I do," I'd promised myself that I would do everything in my power to be the best wife I could be. After all, I was living my life by Proverbs 31:25-26, "Strength and honor are her clothing; and she shall rejoice in time to come. She opens her mouth with wisdom; and in her tongue is the law of kindness." I wanted and needed to be an example to the young women who were coming behind me. Someone had to stand strong and fight for marriages that would inspire our young people.

I couldn't name one person my age or younger who had a successful marriage—a successful marriage that didn't have its struggles. Sure, my girl Lashawn and her husband had gone through some things, but they had managed to talk it out and come out on top. They were going on their second year of marriage. Even though I'd never had a strong example in my family to follow, I planned to make my own, showing my son and daughter that every good thing is worth fighting for. Just because things are not going your way, doesn't mean you give up and walk away. You just have to find a way to make it work, trust that things will and can get better, and trouble doesn't last always.

That day as he was driving to me to school, I thought about some of the things we'd discussed earlier that week. It was so hard for me to swallow my pride, but I reminded myself that marriage is about compromise. I told him that I was going to put my education on hold and focus on our family. I knew that he thought I wasn't giving him and the children enough of my time, so I promised to be more understanding and supportive of his decision, and to put him first before my own needs. I was almost finished with school but I was willing to take a break and work on us. After I finished speaking, he just sat in silence. He eventually broke the quiet by carefully stating that he didn't want me to do that. He insisted that I needed to put my school first and not take any breaks. "You should think about your career.

Stunned, I didn't know what to say. Then an interesting thought crossed my mind and I voiced it. "It sounds like you're telling me that I need to focus on school because you're not planning on being here in the future. I feel like you want to leave me, but you haven't figured out how to do it yet." To this, he replied softly, "I'm sorry, Kessan." I looked at him and said, "Have a nice day." Head held high, I got out of the car. This was not the time for me to let him drive me crazy. It was my last few weeks of school and I had a final exam in my English class that I really needed to pass. I walked away and didn't say another word.

While I sat in class fighting to concentrate and not think about what just happened, I received a text message from him saying that he was sorry for what he'd said and that we were just going through a rough patch, but everything was going to be okay. He continued on by saying that he loved me and that he wanted to make our marriage work. I felt the pain in my heart ease up. But for how long?

Things were okay for the next few days, but Kyle was acting really strange. He never said much. When he'd come home from work, all he wanted to do was sleep. Then he would get up around nine p.m. and go over to his Aunt Joan's house to check on her. It became a routine.

One of my friends from church was having a birthday party. Not expecting him to escort me, I got all dressed up and went with my sister Andrea. Because the tension in my home hadn't really eased up, I decided to have some fun at the party. I danced, laughed, and even had a drink. Everyone was having a nice time. Suddenly, I felt my cell phone vibrating. Curious, I took it out of my purse and saw that it was Kyle. I answered and told him to hold on until I could get to a quiet spot. When I was able to hear him, he told me that he was coming to get me because he wanted me to come home. Smiling, I told him to stay in bed and I would be home in an hour. Racing home, I hurried through the door and he was in bed waiting for me. He pulled back the covers and patted the bed for me to get in. Happy, I quickly put on my pajamas and jumped in, and we held each other and kissed. Finally, the intimacy I'd so longed for. I think the one martini I drank started to get to me. Not wanting to kill the mood, I reluctantly admitted that I was too tired and why, but I wanted him to hold me. I also reminded him that we had to get up early for church, so we should both go to sleep.

The next morning at church, once again Kyle was acting weird. He kept sitting up in his seat, putting his face in his hands, and wasn't really paying attention to the Word that was being preached. I put my arms around him and rubbed his back. Once we got out of church, we decided to get a bite to eat like we always did. Inside the car, I asked him, "What's going on with you?" Finally, he said he had been depressed for a long time, and he didn't know why. Concerned, I asked if I could do something to help him. Shaking his head, he said there was nothing I could do. He just needed time to think some things out. After hearing those words, I told him I wasn't hungry anymore. I just wanted to go home. I knew I couldn't let this get me down. It was Super Bowl weekend and we were supposed to go over to his friend Luther's house to watch the game.

When we got home, I told him to give me a second so I could change my clothes and put on something more comfortable. While I was in the bedroom getting dressed, he came in behind me and said he was thinking that maybe I should stay home and let him go alone since we hadn't been getting along. He didn't want any of our tension to ruin other people's fun. He turned around and called Jamie's name. When she answered, he told her that he was leaving and said if she still wanted to go over to her friend's house, he would drop her off on the way. Shocked into momentary silence, I didn't even get a chance to respond before he grabbed the keys to his aunt's car and left.

Suddenly drained, I just dropped down on my bed in disbelief. I couldn't understand why he would just leave me at home alone with no money or transportation. Allowing myself to give in to the despair, I lay back onto the bed and cried for about two hours straight. I couldn't figure out for the life of me why he was treating me this way. What had I done that was so terrible to make him do this? I didn't know what was going on with him and exactly why was he was so stressed out. Was it because of what the girls' mom was putting him through or had he been talking to Jenifer again? I knew he saw her at work, but I tried not to let that bother me. I was the one he'd married; he'd chosen me after everything we had been through. Besides, she couldn't be that desperate to continue seeing him after he'd left her, came back to me, then made me his wife! Or was she?

I tried not to think of how sad I was, or to allow him to break me down. I just kept telling myself this was only a test and I would pass. Deciding I needed to take my mind off my problems for a bit, I studied for a while, and later watched television until I fell asleep. I woke up when I heard voices coming through the door. I got up quickly from the couch and went into the bedroom to avoid talking to him. I couldn't even tell you when he eventually came to bed because I fell fast asleep as soon as my head hit the pillow. I guess I really wore myself out from all the crying I had done.

The next day, I wasn't my usual upbeat self at school. I didn't want to talk to anyone, and didn't feel like making anyone feel good with my usual words of encouragement. I didn't even stay after class for my study group. All I wanted to do was go back home. The only real bright spot that day was the fact that I didn't have to catch the bus. A friend who lived in my neighborhood offered me a ride home. She wasn't going to her last class, so she drove me home. Initially, I thought about politely declining the ride because I usually liked riding the bus home. It gave me more time to sit with my thoughts and figure things out. But on this particular day, I really wanted to get home fast so I could call Kyle and see if he was feeling any better.

Once I got home, I called him expecting to leave him a message that I was at home and needed to talk, but he actually answered. He didn't sound like he was happy to hear my voice on the phone. In an effort to lighten the mood, I asked him how his day was going and what did he want me to cook for dinner. Instead of answering my questions, he informed me that he had called Pastor White, and we had an appointment to meet with him that day at three-thirty p.m. I was about to ask him for what reason, but I already knew why. I just hung up the phone and watched the time go by, much like watching a snail move from one side of the street to the other. This was unbelievably painful. When I heard him pull up, I ran downstairs and got into the car. He didn't even speak when I got in. I endured the awkward silence the entire trip over to the church. I was extremely relieved when we pulled up and Pastor was at the door waiting for us. We followed him to his office and took a seat.

At first, nobody spoke; then he asked Kyle, "Well, what's going on, son?" Kyle blurted out, "I can't do this anymore. I'm not happy!" My mouth flew open in amazement. I mean I knew we weren't getting along, but for him to actually say that threw me for a loop. Kyle also said that I made him feel like he and the girls were in the way, and he knew I didn't love him the way I should. He proceeded to say we should be having more sex than we were and it was my fault.

Now, that was plain unfair and made me upset because all I had been doing was trying to please him in every way. He was right—we didn't have much intimacy because I was cooking, cleaning, doing homework, watching the girls, helping them with their homework before I could do mine, and giving him the attention I thought he needed when he got home from work. I also needed to take care of my own child, and I was still trying to figure out how all of us would fit in this two-bedroom apartment once Keithshon came home in five months. After taking care of all that, when I finally did get in the bed, he would be fast asleep. So whose fault was it again? As I listened to him bash me, I sat there crying. I felt empty and didn't really know why I was crying, but I felt I needed to at the time. I knew I didn't have any more to give him.

When the meeting concluded, we went home and I made his dinner. The meeting with Pastor had taken a lot out of me. I wanted to be alone so I made a pallet on the couch and slept there for the night. That week went by fast. I kept myself busy with school and the gym. I intentionally stayed out of his way and gave him his space.

On Wednesday night, Kyle explained that he wasn't feeling well. He wanted to stay home and relax; he insisted it wouldn't hurt if we missed Bible study one night. He told me that he was tired of us fighting and he just wanted to start over. We called a truce and fell asleep. The next morning I got up early so I could make it to school on time. I had a paper that I had to turn in and needed to get over to the library to print it out. Since his aunt was letting me take the car, I figured I would go pay some bills after school, do the grocery shopping, come home start dinner, run him a bath, give him some medicine, and put him to bed early, and that's exactly what I did. I felt like things were going to be just fine with us after all.

It was finally Friday. Valentine's Day was that Sunday. I thought maybe that was just what the doctor had ordered for us. I didn't have to go to school so I stayed home and cleaned to make sure I was freed up to enjoy Valentine Day. I wanted to go out that night and just spend some alone time with Kyle. I was having a great day, so when my phone rang and the display on the caller ID printed out "Hubby," I was happy. It had been so long since he called me in the middle of the day just to say hello. I picked the phone up with all this excitement running through my body. He asked how my day was going. I told him good and that I was taking care of the house, and maybe when he got home, we could go have dinner at our favorite soul food restaurant in Long Beach and catch a movie. Instead of agreeing, he said he needed to talk and that he had been thinking about it all day long. Disappointment and hurt replaced my excitement. I took a deep breath and sat down to hear him out.

He started to explain he had been really trying to bring himself out of the depression he was experiencing, but he just couldn't seem to do it. He then went on to say that he had discussed the problem with his aunt. She thought that it might be a mental illness that the men in his family suffered with. He said he was thinking about going to see a doctor. I was thinking he was full of crap, but I told him that it was okay and I would be there for him every step of the way. I promised that we could get through this together. He didn't see it that way. He claimed he needed some time alone to deal with his problems and was going to stay at his aunt's house for a while until he felt better.

Holding on to my Christian principles, I didn't curse him out. I told him that if he was going to do it, then just do whatever it was he needed to do. Honestly, I was fed up with him and all of his back and forth. Disgusted with the games, I slammed the phone down and sat in the dining room with my head down on the table. Around five o'clock, I fell asleep. I didn't think I was sad when I went to bed, but when I kept waking up throughout the night, I knew different. So I sat up and prayed myself back to sleep.

At eight a.m., I heard Kyle coming through the door. He walked into the room and asked me how I was doing. I told him not to say anything to me, just get some clothes, and get out; that's what he did. I knew there was no way I was going back to sleep, so I got up and went for a run, thinking this would make me feel better. I didn't even make it around the first corner before I broke down and started crying. I couldn't stop, so I ran back to the house, went into my room, and closed the door. I didn't want to wake Jamie because she would come in asking me what was wrong. I wasn't ready to bring her into this mess just yet. I wanted to keep her out of it until I had something definite to tell. Needing a friend, I picked up the phone, called Lashawn, and told her everything that had happened. We spent the next two hours on the phone talking and praying through one of the worst moments in my life.

I tried to keep myself busy that whole day but it was hard. I didn't have any transportation, so I couldn't leave the house to take my mind off things. So I did what I always do when I was stressed out and needed to feel better. I put on some music and cleaned my house from top to bottom. Lashawn called me throughout the day to check on me and let me know that she and her husband, Harley, would come by to take me to church in the morning. Her kind gesture took a little of the load off my shoulders. Kyle called and asked me if I wanted him to come to take me to church. I thanked him but rejected his offer, letting him know that I already had a ride, but I would see him there. Hurrying off the phone, I took a nice, hot bath and relaxed for the rest of the evening until I fell asleep. I was surprised when I slept through the night. I guess I was excited, thinking that he would be at church and all this mess would be over.

I got out of bed and went through my normal Sunday morning routine. I turned on the television, put on some coffee, and hopped into the shower. As I was getting out, I thought I heard my phone ring. I rushed into the room and saw that I had a missed call from Kyle. I decided that I wasn't going to call him back. I already had a feeling it was going to be something I didn't want to hear. The Spirit had already told me that he wasn't going to show up.

I kept getting ready for church and he called back. As I looked at the phone and watched his name flash across the screen, I hesitated before answering, but I did. On the last ring, I answered and heard him say, "Hello" twice. I asked, "What do you need?" He paused for a few seconds then said he was not going to make it to church because he didn't feel right coming. Plus, he didn't want people asking him questions. Then I asked him if he was seriously going to leave me at church by myself on Valentine's Day? He replied, "I can't do it!" and hung up. All day, people kept asking me where he was. This was the second week that he hadn't come to church. So, I did what anyone else would have done: I lied and said that he was at home sick, and that he would be there next week.

When I returned home after church, I was sad. This was a special day when couples exhibited their love for each other, but I was coming home to any empty house. How could this have happened to me? I thought I had done everything right, but bad things just kept happening, no matter how much of a good person I tried to be. I would pray, fast, love, and I forgave people when they hurt me. Lord, why is it that I'm always the one getting hurt? I took off my shoes, left them by the front door, and headed to my bedroom to lie down. When I walked inside, I saw a card and a bear on my pillow. I picked up the card and read, "No matter what happens, just know that I will always love you." My heart softened; even after I'd told myself that I wasn't going to call him no matter what, I went back on my own word and called him.

The phone rang twice before Kyle answered. I greeted him back and asked how he was feeling. He said he was fine, about to leave to go out to eat with his aunt. Then it came out. I asked him why he wasn't with me on Valentine's Day and expressed that we should be spending this time together. He didn't even bother to answer. Instead of saying, "O.k., you're right," he used reverse psychology and said, "You know what? I have been sitting in this house, crying my eyes out because I don't know what's wrong with me. I haven't come out my room and I have to make myself eat. Now you have pushed me right back into that corner I've been trying to get out of for days. All I want to do is just curl up in a ball and die, so I'm getting off the phone with you because I can't talk to you anymore. You always make it about you." I sat there with tears streaming down my face, just looking at the phone. I let the phone slide to the floor, fell down next to it, and cried like a baby for hours. I cried so long and hard that after awhile I couldn't even cry anymore.

I prayed to God all night asking him to give me supernatural strength to help me get through the embarrassment of this situation. I also asked the Lord how I was going to show my face at church. What were people going to say? Who gets married then her husband leaves two months later, two days before Valentine's Day? Lashawn kept calling me to check on me, but I didn't want to talk. I needed to be alone. After lying on the floor for over six hours, I decided to get in my bed to try to fall asleep.

I woke up the next morning and couldn't get out of bed. I knew that I had to get Jamie up and I couldn't miss class. Besides, I didn't want to stay home alone. I knew I needed to be around other people. So I got up and threw on the first thing I saw, walked eight blocks to the bus stop, and headed to school. I noticed that when I was outside, I didn't think much about my situation. It was only when the professor I worked for on campus asked me how was I feeling that I thought about it. She already knew what I was going through because days prior, I'd broken down and started crying for no reason in her office.

Needing to share and talk to someone who didn't know him, I'd told her my situation. Although I wasn't seeking comforting words, she did make me feel better after our discussion. That's why I needed to be there. I even stayed late after work just so I didn't have to go home. I knew I was neglecting Jamie, but at that moment, I needed to be alone. I was of no use to her in my condition.

Pastor White's seventieth birthday was coming up and his children were throwing him a big surprise birthday party. I was asked to minister in dance. I wanted to say no, but this man was like my own father and had always been there for me. Even when I knew he was tired or not feeling well, he never failed me. That was the least I could do, put my pride aside and do this for him. Once again, I wondered how I was going to explain Kyle's absence. He had missed two weeks in a row, and I knew that I wasn't going to be able to get away with the story about him being sick anymore. I knew that I was either going to have to stay away from everyone that night, lie again, or say forget it and tell them the truth. They were bound to find out sooner or later anyway. So when one of the elders walked over to my table and asked where Kyle was, instead of going with my first thought and saying he was at home sick, I told her, "I don't have a clue. I haven't seen him in two weeks, but if you see him, please tell him hello for me." I truly didn't mean for it to come out that way, but I was bitter and I felt this was the perfect time to put it out there that he'd left me. She didn't seem shocked. She told me that she'd had a dream that I'd come to her and asked her to pray for us because Kyle was up to his old ways again. The look in her eyes told me that she was sincere, and at that moment, I felt a little relief. I didn't have to carry this secret around any longer. Little did I know, the words of John 8:32 were going to give me a freedom I'd never known.

I rode with my godbrother Daniel to the birthday party. I knew that he would make me laugh, and even though he was only twenty-three years old, this young man had so much wisdom. He would always set me straight and tell it like it was. He didn't care if it hurt my feelings because he knew I would respect the truth and move on from there. He also kept my mind off everything going on. We pulled up to the venue; he dropped me off at the front door, and went to park the car. As I walked in, I found Lashawn and Harley, and sat at their table. I was happy we were in the back; that way I was out of sight.

As the night progressed, more and more people started making their way over. No matter how hard I tried not to make eye contact, someone always found a way to get my attention. I found myself saying all night, "Oh, he still isn't feeling well; please just keep us in your prayers." It was finally time to get dressed, so I went into the ladies' room, put on my praise dance clothes, and said a prayer like I always did. My mind was very clear because I'd been fasting all day, which was something I'd done whenever I had to minister. I put my things down and took my place. Since I was asked to do this for his birthday, I picked a song that not only addressed the occasion, but also ministered to my situation at that moment, *Thank You* by Smokie Norful. Boy, I had so much to thank Him for.

In the beginning, it was hard. I couldn't seem to let down my guard and allow the Holy Spirit in; the more I pushed, the more I let go. The next thing I knew all eyes were glued on me. It was as though everyone was watching me push the layers of pain off me. When I was done, I was very close to empty. I hadn't let it all go, but I'd left a large part of myself in that dance. When I came back into the restroom, Lashawn was waiting for me with tears in her eyes; she said she couldn't believe what she had seen and how much of a blessing it was to her. I thanked her because that was all I wanted to do, be a blessing to everyone. Sometimes you have to step outside of yourself to let that happen. Back at the table, I still didn't want to talk to anyone. I wanted to leave and I told Daniel to take me home.

Once I got home, I sat on my bench in the dining room and had a bowl of cereal. I tried to go to sleep after my shower, but I just wasn't tired. I sat up for hours thinking about what people were probably saying about me. I wondered if they knew that Kyle had left me, and after awhile, I didn't want to think any more. I eventually turned off all the lights, lay down in the living room, and fell asleep. This seemed to be the only place in the house I could fall asleep. My bedroom was a cold and lonely reminder of my failing marriage.

I loved getting up and getting on the bus. I found that I paid attention to everything around me. I was able to watch the people and wonder about their stories rather than obsess about mine. I finished my English and History classes, so I picked up a Writing class that was only four weeks long. I would sit on the bus and study the whole way to school, but on my way back home, I would fall back into a depression. Back to the reality of my life.

As I walked from the bus stop heading home, I started to talk to God and asked him what I was supposed to do. I didn't want Kyle to have this control over my life. I needed to go and file for a divorce. Every time I tried to mention it, I would hear a voice saying not to, just stand and pray. Up until this point, I wasn't angry, just very hurt. When I heard the voice telling me to stand and pray, that's when I got mad at God. I asked Him, "How do you expect for me to pray for this marriage? Pray for what? Why should I have to pray for him? He was the one who had weaseled his way back into my life, lying to everyone who would listen. Talking about how God told him that I was his wife. Why should I pray for a cheater, a man who needed to burn in hell for all the hurt he'd has caused me and many others? I'm not doing anything for this man and he can drop dead for all I care. All I want is for him to fix my car; then we will never have to say a word to each other ever in life."

I walked all the way home with my earphones on because I didn't want to hear God's voice any longer. I tuned him out. When I got into the house, Jamie was already home. I started dinner, took my shower, did homework, and went to bed early. I thought when I woke up that all of the thoughts in my head would be gone, but they were still there. I tried not to listen.

I decided that I would take it a step further, and I wasn't going to wear my wedding ring. I took it off and threw it in my jewelry box. As soon as I tried to walk away, a voice told me to put it back on. Now I tried desperately not to listen, but then I heard it again, "You are still a married woman and you can't do what he does. Put your ring back on." I walked back to my room with tears in my eyes and put my ring back on my finger. I knew that this was going to be a bad day for me. I walked to the bus stop that morning with my head down and glasses on because I felt that if I even made eye contact with anyone that day, they would see the pain in my soul. I made sure I stayed to myself. I even left early and skipped work, which was something I never did.

For the next two weeks, I fasted and prayed. I had a book that my sister Andrea had given on my wedding day titled, *The Power of a Praying Wife* by Stormie Omartian. I'd thought about giving it back because when I opened it and read the first page I thought to myself, *I'm not going to need this.* Kyle and I had been through enough to know how to overcome and deal with our problems. I was in the house praying and saw the book. I picked it up and started to read it. Not only was it talking about how to pray, stand, and give your problemed husband to the Lord, but it had prayers for generational curses and how to break to them.

After reading that book, I made it a point to do a complete fast, no food at all for three days. I would have liquids only. I had done this before, so I knew it wouldn't be hard. After I came off my fast, I was waiting to hear from God, but still nothing happened. I fasted again the next week and still nothing. After my third fast and still no word, I was convinced that God had forgotten about me. I mean, He was the one telling me not to take off my ring. Every time I wanted to call and curse Kyle out, I would hear the Lord tell me not to say a mumbling word. The only reason I'd wanted to say hurtful things to Kyle was I needed him to hurt as bad as I was hurting. But it wouldn't help. Instead of cursing him, I was to pray for him, and then I remembered the scriptures that talked about "pray for those who despitefully use you," Matthew 5:44. "If you hold your peace then I will fight your battle," Numbers 12:1-15. So that's what I did. I humbled myself with tears in my eyes, fell to my knees, and started worshipping God and praying. Before I knew it, two hours had passed and I was on the floor, face down. I was so tired from praying that I crawled into my room, closed my door, and stayed in there for the rest of the night. I had to keep the faith that one day soon I would hear a word from God, but until then I would do the best I could to keep living my life and not give up.

I couldn't believe it had been two months and Easter was coming up. I should be happy. I hadn't missed a Sunday at church yet. But on this Sunday, I couldn't pull myself together to get out of bed. I didn't want to go to the sunrise service; I couldn't make myself do it. I didn't think the holiday would be so hard. This was a day when families would be together cooking, eating, and laughing. The thought of this sent me right back into my depression.

Easter morning I pulled the covers over my head and planned to stay there the whole day. I already knew that it wouldn't be long before everyone would come looking for me. As soon as church let out, my phone started to ring off the hook. Everyone was calling asking where I was, if I was okay, and why I hadn't come to church. They even said my pastor kept asking where his daughter was. I didn't care about anything. I turned off my phone and rolled over in my bed.

As soon as I thought the coast was clear, my doorbell rang. Then it rang again. I tried to act as if I wasn't home. Whoever was at the door wouldn't go away, so Jamie finally got out the bed and opened it. When I heard her say, "Hey, aunties," I knew it was Christina, Angie, and Andrea. My sisters let themselves in my room, but I still refused to move. So they all sat around me, grabbed hands, and started to pray; tears streamed down my face. I couldn't stop them from flowing then they all just hugged me and we sat there in silence.

I didn't plan to get out of bed that day, but my sisters thought it would be a good idea to cook. While I remained in my room, they all went to the store, bought food, and cooked dinner. I was in a dark mood, and I wished that they would leave and let me be alone. Once I smelled the ham, mac and cheese, candied yams, and cabbage cooking, I started to feel better. I got out of bed, put on my robe, and went and sat at the kitchen table where they were talking and laughing. I didn't say much, I just sat there and looked out the window until it was time for dinner.

I told myself that I wasn't going to call Kyle at all. I wanted all this to go away. Somewhere in the back of my mind, I thought this was all a dream, and soon I would wake up and still be married. I knew that as a Christian woman I was supposed to fight for my marriage. I had walked away from my first marriage and never looked back. I had always regretted that decision. I had never tried to fight for Shawn and I didn't pray, trust, or believe we could work. I just gave up. I knew that this time I had to do the right thing.

One afternoon, I got home from school and decided to pick up my phone and call Kyle. After the first two rings, I wanted to hang up, but then he answered. I said to him, "Hey, how are you?" He responded, "Fine, doing a lot better." He elaborated and explained how his battle with depression was lifting and he was doing better. He was finally starting to get some of his joy back. Hearing this brought a little smile to my face because his reason for leaving was his sudden sadness and stress. I admitted to being happy that he was feeling better. Then there was an awkward silence. I could tell he wasn't going to talk so I just took a leap of faith and said, "So when are you coming home?" He quickly stated, "I'm not," to which I declared, "What do you mean you're not coming home? You said you needed time to yourself to get your mind together and then things would be okay. What about this marriage?" That's when he retorted, "I don't want it anymore! I'm not happy and I think we should just let it go. I don't want to be married anymore."

After being with him all these years and dealing with his going back and forth, I still couldn't wrap my head around what he was saying. As I sat on the floor thinking, *How do you go from chasing someone for a year and a half, tell them that you can't rest until you get them back, to being married for two months then all of a sudden have this big epiphany that you don't want to be married anymore?* Refusing to even try to understand his way of thinking, I ended the conversation with, "Well, you take care of yourself, and I pray you have a good life." I hung up the phone and didn't look back.

A few weeks passed and even though I wanted to run to the courthouse to file for a divorce, I knew I couldn't do anything until I heard a Word from God. I decided to put this behind me for a while. Two mouths passed and still not one word from Kyle. I was driving home on the freeway with the window down with no music playing. I was enjoying the fact that my car was repaired and it was a beautiful day.

For the first time in months, I had peace. Then all of a sudden, I heard a voice so clearly I could have sworn there was someone in the car sitting next to me talking. The voice stopped as suddenly as it started. I sat there driving with my mouth wide open. I absolutely couldn't believe what I just heard. I guess not thinking about my situation for a few days allowed my mind to clear so I could hear the Lord. That is why it shook me to my very core when I heard His voice clear as a bell.

"I told you that this wasn't your husband a long time ago, but you wouldn't listen. So when he came back into your life professing that I had sent him, you took his word over Mine. Even though you doubted, you still didn't come to Me and ask if this was true. That is why you felt the way you did about it the whole time. You wanted to believe it, so I stood back and let it come to pass. I knew that he would do what he did; that is why I gave you that dream a few days after your marriage. Don't you recall the dream where he left you on the road somewhere and never came back? I was preparing you for what was to come. Yes, on your wedding day it was perfect because I stepped back. I also told you that you needed to get married fast because all of this had to happen now. What I have for you is so much greater. I needed to show you who he was, once and for all, so he couldn't ever come back into your life. I let this happen so that you would finally see him for who he is—a wolf in sheep's clothing. This was not your husband and never could have been, but the only way for Me to show you was to let you go through this and never look back. Your ending will be much greater than you're beginning. Trust in Me and not man." That is when I heard that it was time.

I couldn't believe what had just happened. It was so powerful that I didn't tell anyone for a while, but when I got the okay to file for my divorce, I called my pastor and explained to him what had happened and that I was going to go ahead with the divorce. Pastor White told me that as long as I had heard from the Lord, he would back my decision. The next morning, I went down to the courthouse and filed my paperwork. I did something that I hadn't done in months. I smiled! I had finally gotten my joy back.

Later that night, I sat outside thinking about all that had happened in the past few weeks, and it hit me! I now understood why the entire time I was going through my engagement and the marriage, I just wasn't as excited as I should have been. I couldn't quite comprehend it then. Now, I can see how God was protecting me even back then. I felt so bad when I thought about how I wanted to be married, just not to him. I kept wondering why I couldn't love him the way I used to. All this time, I thought it was my fault for him leaving. Even when I cried, it was never because I missed him. Simply put, I wanted him back because I was thinking about the humiliation it caused me, how I was going to have to face the people at church. Yet, the Lord was doing a great work the whole time and now I have peace about it all.

After nine months, I am at peace with myself, and more importantly, my God. I graduated from college in June of 2011, with my AA in psychology. My divorce was finalized in February. I am doing well. I have friends around me who mean well and are trying to fix me up on blind dates all the time. They love to tell me that the best way to get over a man is to get another one. I know better than that. At this juncture in my life, I want to focus on what is good for me. I know I will never be good to, or for, any man until I learn how to really love myself and fix all the issues I have carried from my childhood. This is best achieved by therapy, prayer, and being alone. I have to get to know Kessan, and figure out why I always fall into the same type of relationships. Was it me or was it them?

Me and Keithshon

Me (3rd from left) and my sisters.

Me and Jamie

Chapter Eight:
The Battle Is Not Yours; It's the Lord's.

After being alone for almost a year, I started to get a clear understanding of why I fell into certain traps. I was always looking for love from man instead of from God. I'd trusted everything that they'd told me and would take them back every time they cheated or lied. God's word says trust in Him and not in the things of this world—like cars, clothes, money, or man. I would even date them knowing they were with other women. Like many silly women, I foolishly believed that if I could take them from their girlfriends, then I was better than them. Boy, talking about being screwed up! My abandonment issues made me believe that I was unworthy of being loved. Instead of letting a bad man go, I would put up with his mess, naively hoping that they would realize I was a good woman and get it together. But we see how that turned out.

I wish I could tell you what happens next, but I don't have a clue myself. I'm excited to see what God has in store, where the Lord is leading me. I have always wondered why I was born and why my life has been full of heartache and pain, but once I gave my life to God and started to fully trust Him with every area of my life, He began to show me things that I could never have imagined in my wildest dreams. I know that everything I have been through was never about me, but for those I have to help down the road. Yes, sometimes I feel as though my burdens are heavy and that they weigh me down to where I can't even move, but God will never put more on me than I can bear. Thus, I have no choice but to push through every storm and come out on top.

I may never fully comprehend why God allowed me to go through so much pain and shed so many tears, but I have learned to just shut up and know "to whom much is given, much will be required," Luke 12:48. That is why the devil has been trying to take me out since day one. There are three things that are certain in life: you are either going through a storm, coming out of one, or getting ready for one. I pray that every young, middle-aged, or elderly person reading this book understands that no matter what you have been through, or are going through at the moment, God has your back. True, you might want to give up right now and throw in the towel, but know that you have to keep pushing because your breakthrough will occur when things seem like they can't get any worse. That's when you know God is up to something. You can't have "monies" without the test, that's how we get our "testimonies" (Pastor Sanders White, Sr.). So keep standing and keep praying no matter how it looks. Please know that it's never just about you, but it is also about those you can help along the way. I pray that you will all be blessed and encouraged, and remember that God has not given us the spirit of fear, but love, power and a sound mind (2 Timothy 1:7).

As for me, I am just waiting to see what God has in store for me. Before I gave my life over to God, I never believed that I was worthy of love. Now I know better.